Tell Me a Story about
    This Crazy World Called
High School

Tell Me a Story about This Crazy World Called

High School

A Survival Guide for Adolescence

MRS. D.

Illustrated by Tara Balboa

TELL ME A STORY ABOUT THIS CRAZY WORLD CALLED HIGH SCHOOL
A SURVIVAL GUIDE FOR ADOLESCENCE

iUniverse books may be ordered through booksellers or by contacting:

iUniverse
1663 Liberty Drive
Bloomington, IN 47403
www.iuniverse.com
1-800-Authors (1-800-288-4677)

Because of the dynamic nature of the Internet, any web addresses or links contained in this book may have changed since publication and may no longer be valid. The views expressed in this work are solely those of the author and do not necessarily reflect the views of the publisher, and the publisher hereby disclaims any responsibility for them.

Any people depicted in stock imagery provided by Thinkstock are models, and such images are being used for illustrative purposes only. Certain stock imagery © Thinkstock.

ISBN: 978-1-4917-8891-2 (sc)
ISBN: 978-1-4917-8892-9 (e)

Library of Congress Control Number: 2016901907

Print information available on the last page.

iUniverse rev. date: 06/14/2016

To my students, thank you for sharing your stories. You are an inspiration!

To my parents and guardians, thank you for believing in your children. Love always wins!

To my colleagues, thank you for choosing the greatest
profession. You have the power to change lives!

To my administrators, thank you for an opportunity of a lifetime! I am forever grateful.

To my family and friends, thank you for your support—today, tomorrow, and forever!

Preface

Tell Me a Story about This Crazy World Called High School began evolving several years ago when I was going through a slow and silent metamorphosis from an elementary teacher to a high school counselor.

There is one extremely emotional day that remains etched in my mind forever. The sun was shining that warm summer's day. My cousin and I were leisurely walking toward a diner on Northern Boulevard in Jackson Heights, New York. The past few hours had been consumed by cleaning fifty years of memories from our grandparents' house. That house now stood empty and silent. In that special house, the sound of laughter and music had always prevailed; the love of family had abounded; and our strong appreciation of the arts, theater, and storytelling had been nurtured.

On that day, my cousin asked me one very important question about my book—"Who will your audience be?"

I felt overwhelmed and said, "Who am I writing for? Why would I spend so many hours writing a book about adolescence when there are hundreds of books already written?" I wasn't certain whom I was going to share these deepest thoughts with, but I listened to my inner voice. I continued listening. I continued typing. As time went on, and as each young person shared his or her story with me, the answer became very clear. My audience would be you, that very special someone.

Someone—
Someone who is an adolescent,
Someone who is going to be an adolescent,
Someone who has gone through adolescence,
Someone who is raising an adolescent,
Someone who is teaching an adolescent,
And especially
Someone who thinks that
He or she is alone in adolescence,
Please know that you are not alone.
Please know that there is hope.
Please know that life is worth living.
Please know that the sun will shine tomorrow,
If only you believe in you!

Introduction

Tell Me a Story about This Crazy World Called High School speaks to the adolescent, the parent/guardian of the adolescent, and the teacher of the adolescent. It is my hope to alleviate some fears that have resounded over and over again while I've counseled hundreds of high school students. (Please know that there is always hope. Please know that you are never alone.)

After countless hours of listening to students, parents/guardians, and teachers, I created a book to allow everyone involved in this chaotic time to gain a better understanding of the world of adolescence. In order to capture the emotional, social, and academic development that occurs throughout teen years, I divided it into three distinct parts.

Part 1, "High School: A World unto Itself," allows the reader to delve into the minds of fifty anonymous teenagers.

- A total of sixty individual stories are presented. The stories are separated by grade level. Two-thirds of the writers are female. One-third of the writers are male.
- A variety of topics are unraveled as each vulnerable teen reveals his or her soul. They range from the simplest (a fight with a friend) to the most complex (thoughts of suicide).
- Some stories were written in times of crisis, and others were written during more peaceful times. (An asterisk denotes that a story was written in a time of crisis.)
- A brief question or statement preceding each piece of writing provides insight into the world of each individual adolescent.
- A small character with a lightbulb appears after each story. (If the words touch your heart, draw what you are feeling.)
- A journal titled "Tell Me Your Story" follows each writing sample. It gives you an opportunity to write your feelings. (Writing helps heal the soul.)

Part 2, "A Survival Guide for Adolescents, Parents/Guardians, and Teachers of Adolescents," consists of several writing exercises that allow for self-reflection and personal growth.

- "Surviving Adolescence" begins with the definition of adolescence, parenting, and teaching. It continues with a bill of rights and ends with some practical coping skills developed to help everyone survive these tumultuous years.
- "Life's Toughest Questions" responds to the topics discussed in the sixty anonymous adolescent writings. There is no one solution to all of life's problems. There is no one perfect fit to solve the complexities of life, yet there is one simple answer to help begin the healing process: love.
- "Introspection" speaks to your inner thoughts and emotions. It is divided into two sections. The first segment is devoted to the adolescent. The second segment is dedicated to the adult. It searches deep within your soul. (Please be honest with yourself. If you need to talk to someone, please reach out for help.)

Part 3, "Afterthoughts," contains a collection of poetry and prose written to students, parents/guardians, and you. (Sometimes the written word has a greater impact than the spoken word.)

Your aspirations are your possibilities.
—Samuel Johnson

Contents

Topics

Abuse   Academics   Addiction   Anger

Anxiety   Choices   Death   Divorce

Drugs   Family   Fear   Future

Hope   Life   Love   Trust

Faith   Relationships   Respect

Stress   Tolerance

Characters

Adolescents

Parents/Guardians

Teachers

Respect yourself and others will respect you.
—Confucius

Part 1

High School: A World unto Itself

A journey of a thousand miles begins with a single step.
—Lao Tzu

Initially, *Tell Me a Story about This Crazy World Called High School* contained a collection of "Dear Me" stories written by adolescents, ages thirteen through eighteen, who were engulfed in the throes of what to them were the most serious crises of the day. (Think back to your adolescent years. Remember those feelings!) Each person sat in the same chair in my office, facing the same wall, crying the same tears, and feeling the same desperation. Each one was searching for hope, love, the meaning of life, or happiness.

As a counselor, I listened empathetically, without judgment. I silently sorted out the array of emotions that were so overpowering. Inevitably, someone would knock on my door at the most crucial moment. I would grab a piece of paper and a pencil and ask the tearful teen to write exactly what was going on in his or her mind. Several of the writings that follow were written during times of crisis. An asterisk at the beginning of a writing piece denotes that it was written with tears. The passages portray students' innermost thoughts and feelings buried deep within. Names have been changed, but the heartfelt words remain intact.

As time went on, hundreds of adolescents continued to sit in that same chair, facing that same wall, but something was different. There were no tears. There was no crisis (at the moment). There was no pain (at the moment). They were happy and smiling (at the moment), yet I heard them speak of the same struggles. They were searching for love, the meaning of life, or happiness.

They were living in this crazy world called adolescence. How were they surviving? What were they thinking and feeling? What were their coping skills? I asked them if they would share their stories. Within a day, a week, or a month, I graciously received their personal writings: essays, poetry, and journals. These writings were done in the comfort of their own homes—peacefully and quietly. They contained their innermost thoughts and feelings.

I am forever grateful to all those who have chosen to write. Your words may just be what another teen needs to hear.

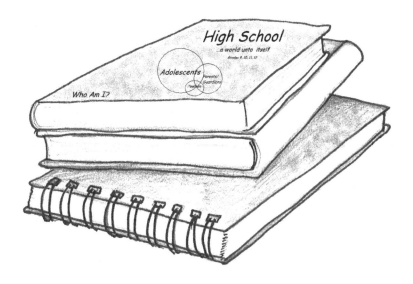

Freshman Year
Lend Me a Hand

T
e
l
l

M
e

Y
o
u
r

S
t
o
r
y

*Freshman Girl
Feeling Upset

This beautiful young girl came crying to my office. She wanted to stay strong. A boy's words were trying to destroy her, but would they?

Dear Me,

I am really hurt by this boy. I feel like a girl who has no friends to protect her. I feel upset because someone is letting me down when I'm feeling good about myself. I just want a friend by my side. This person is not nice. I ask him nicely to stop, but he keeps going on about how I am using people.

I feel really mad, and I just can't let anyone else ruin my life because he doesn't have a life. I am a nice, sensitive, beautiful, and smart girl. I just want people to feel the way I do. He's telling me that I'm not good at baseball. He's telling me I'm ugly and fat. He says that I can't get a boyfriend 'cause I'm so retarded. He says that I use people and that I have no friends and no life at all. He sticks his middle finger up at me. He says there is nothing wrong with me and that I am not hurt. He asks me for answers for his work like everything is okay.

T
e
l
l

M
e

y
o
u
r

S
t
o
r
y

*Freshman Girl
Feeling Sad

In the midst of tears, this very emotional young girl shared three poems she had written the night before. Please find her other writings titled *What I Wish to Be to You* and *The One*.

Misunderstood

When I say that I am fine,
Am I really truly fine?
When I smile, does it mean
I'm okay to you?
When I turn away from help,
Does it mean I need you more than ever?
When my eyes tear up,
Does it mean I'm lost?
When I look at you,
Can you tell I'm not fine?
When I hold on tightly to your hands
I wonder if you know that I need a friend.

Tell Me Your Story

Freshman Boy
Feeling Emotional

A very insightful young boy shared an extremely emotional poem written in English class. He was asked to reflect on this very disturbing topic. He is not a victim of abuse. If you are a victim, tell someone who will listen. Get help now!

No Excuse

You hear me crying throughout the night.
The more you hit me, the more I'm in fright.
You hit me so hard I have bruises everywhere.
That goes to show how much you really care.
You say you love me, but I don't believe.
Why in the world would you conceive?
You can see the tears rolling down my face.
Why, oh why, did you bring me into this horrible place?
My greatest fear is that someday I'll be
Just like the person who has done this to me.
The pain you inflict gets worse and worse.
Pretty soon you'll be watching me get put into a hearse.
Sooner or later, I'll be dead.
I wonder if it's tears that you will shed.
Please stop the child abuse!
There is absolutely no excuse!

T
e
l
l

M
e

Y
o
u
r

S
t
o
r
y

*Freshman Girl
Feeling Alone

What makes this beautiful brown-eyed girl so strong?

Something I'm Not

I never try to be something I'm not,
Even though many people don't like me a lot.
And I know many people think I'm real tough,
But sometimes life—it just gets so rough.
Constantly getting judged for the things I do.
Every day, there are so many things that I have to go through.
And sometimes I can't help but break down and cry,
With no one there to wipe the tear that falls from my eye.
But over the years, I've learned to be strong,
To try to be optimistic when things go wrong.
I realize I'm only human.
I can make mistakes too.
I'll continue to succeed in life.
Make myself proud—
That's what I'll proceed to do.

Tell Me Your Story

Freshman Girl
Feeling Outspoken

Will this very sensitive and kind young girl allow anyone to know who she really is?

What I Wish to Be to You

Don't need tears—
Can be better off without them.
But can be as hard as a rock
Where I stand.
Soft to the touch,
Gentle enough to smile,
Proud enough to stand up
And shout out my beliefs.
Caring enough to listen,
Strong enough to hold your hand
When you feel like crawling.
All the above is what I wish to be to you.
Not a prodigy or famous,
Just your normal schoolgirl speaking her mind
Because she knows what's right.
Time after time,
She asks that famous question:
Why?
And she sits and replies to herself,
"The world shall never know."

Tell Me your Story

Freshman Boy
Feeling Hopeful

Can he be the one to change the world?

I Believe

I believe that one day
we will put down our hatred.
I believe that one day the evil that roams
around this earth will vanish for good.
I believe that one day people will put their guns downs
and unite as one.
I believe that one day kids will be able to
walk the streets without fear.
I believe that one day we will all change
for a better tomorrow.
I believe that one day we will all love and
heal one another.
I believe that Obama is a big step that we need
to change.
I believe that the years coming are going to
get easier.
I believe that one day men will learn to love
our women before we regret it.
I believe that we should never take life for granted;
as quick as it comes, it vanishes quicker.
I believe that we can achieve anything
we put our minds to.
I believe that one day the KKK will put down
their burning crosses and love thy brother.
I believe that we can change.
I believe that I can be the spark that
can change the world.

T
e
l
l

M
e

y
o
u
r

S
t
o
r
y

Freshman Boy
Feeling Compassionate

The good old days helped this caring fourteen-year-old boy survive being bullied during elementary school. (Maybe that is why he wrote the previous poem about being the spark to change the world!)

The Good Old Days

Playing with cars as a little kid,
Watching cartoons like *Blue's Clues*,
Never getting into any trouble,
Buying toys from Toys R Us,
Playing cards with my grandma,
Enjoying summers with my nephews,
Listening to hip-hop for the first time,
Kindergarten kids and trips,
Riding my scooter to the Hudson River,
Visiting the Empire State Building,
Being in the city,
Playing baseball on the sidewalk,
Trips to Burger King and others every day,
Playing on the basketball courts by the pier,
Going to the playgrounds around town,
People all over the streets on the Fourth of July,
Watching fireworks from my rooftop,
House shaking every time trucks pass by,
The afternoon traffic on weekdays,
Playing on the school playground,
And watching the world go by—
The days when life was easy.
Yeah, those were the good old days.

T
e
l
l

M
e

Y
o
u
r

S
t
o
r
y

Freshman Boy
Feeling Positive

We can all learn a lesson from this exceptional young boy's outlook on life!

Dear Me,

Being a freshman—not an easy task, most will say. But think about that for a moment. What does that "most" consist of? Adults—moms, dads, aunts, uncles, grandfathers, grandmothers, brothers, and sisters—the list goes on and on. The point I'm trying to make is that these people haven't a clue. Okay, maybe that's a little cruel. I just mean they don't have a clue about freshmen. "Watch out for those seniors!" "You're going to get lost!" "You're going to be scared!" These are phrases commonly heard. But put everyone else aside and listen here now. Listen to a true freshman.

Well, let me tell you a little about myself. I'm _____, fifteen years old, who's starting fresh at _____High School. I'm not a fictional character, I'm not famous, and I'm not invincible. I'm a normal, average freshman just like you. Starting a new school is never easy, but it can be easy if you make it. You'll probably run into bullies, mean teachers, hard tests, and homework you don't like, but just remember that it's not the end of the world. It'll be okay.

My motto is to always have a positive attitude. What's your hobby … sports, art, literature, etc.? Think about that throughout your day. Thinking about playing football or reading a book after school can keep your mood up throughout the day. Keep a list of favorites, like foods or movies or games. They can help your day too. Making friends is also a good idea. There's nothing better than sharing a joke and laughing with someone you can relate with.

Now, you're probably saying, "Well, I've got friends, and I try to keep a good mood, but I have much more serious problems that I deal with." Fine. I truly have only one word for these problems: talk. Talk to your guidance counselor, your parents, your relatives, your friends. Be the chatterbox that's lurking inside of you. And trust me—talking always works. Bully bothering you? Talk to him or her or someone who can prevent them from pestering you. Teacher being mean and giving hard work? Talk to a parent or a guidance counselor. Maybe they can switch you out of that class. Homework piercing your brain? Talk to a friend. They may be able to help you. Remember you'll have plenty of other things to be concerned with in the future. Don't blow your years throughout high school. Don't wreck your childhood. Don't learn to cope with fear. In the words of Doc Brown, "If you put your mind to it, you can accomplish anything."

I'm no miracle worker. I'm no god. I'm not a problem solver. I'm a sharer, a person who shares his thoughts to help others, a person who has dreams like everyone else, and a person who aspires to be in the movie industry. Going to high school makes it that much easier to make your dreams come true.

Me

Tell Me your Story

Sophomore Year
Hold on Tight

Tell

Me

Your

Story

*Sophomore Boy
Feeling Angry

Does he really hate people? What makes him so angry? Only those he allows into his world truly know him. He is a very intelligent, kind, funny, and talented young boy who will succeed in life.

Dear Me,

Who am I? I'm a person, a regular person with different thoughts than anyone else. My musical choice is strange. So, I'm ridiculed for that. I watch anime. I play video games. I watch sports. I eat, sleep, and go to school. I hate people. I hate whatever ticks me off in any way. I'd rather be with my games and videos. My friends come from all over America. They aren't so bad. I miss the old days. I guess I'm just me: someone who thinks and feels differently than all the mindless fools who parade around like they're big.

Tell Me Your Story

27

Sophomore Girl
Feeling Confused

She decided to break up with her boyfriend of two years the previous day. She needed a break. The following is a note that she left on my desk.

Mrs. D.

Yesterday I called Bobby and we just talked about everything that happened. I know by my gut feeling that I couldn't last without being with him because I do care about him so much. I just need to hang out with other people, I guess, to find myself and see what I want and need. I talked to Joe and told him I'm going back with Bobby, and he was so upset. He couldn't understand why, so I explained really good. The conclusion is that we could still hang out. I will wait for him if he gets into trouble after school ... 'cause I'm going to live up to what we call each other: best friends. I think that's best. So what do you think? I'll talk to you later. Have a great day.

Love,
Me

T

e

l

l

M

e

y

o

u

r

S

t

o

r

y

Sophomore Girl
Feeling Insightful

This very mature sophomore shares her words of wisdom about life.

Life

Life is like being in a car.
Those hills and ditches that you come across
On the road called "life" are only the beginning.
There are many more head-on collisions to face ahead.
Sometimes we make wrong turns,
But if you keep your headlights on,
You will see everything clearer and clearer as you go.
Hold on … for the ride of your life.
Undecided and unsure of where you'll end up:
Your final destination.

T
e
l
l

M
e

Y
o
u
r

S
t
o
r
y

*Sophomore Girl
Feeling Confused

She wrote to her mom after one of many arguments. Love always wins!

The One

Standing face to face,
Should I run?
Eye to eye,
Should I look away?
Shouting at me,
Should I scream back?
Tears in your eye,
Should I hold you?
You're mad now,
What can I do?
Because the truth is
I love you!
More than
You will ever know.

Tell Me your Story

_____
_____
_____
_____
_____
_____
_____
_____
_____
_____
_____
_____
_____
_____
_____
_____
_____
_____
_____
_____
_____
_____
_____
_____

Sophomore Girl
Feeling Precious

Writing poetry helped to heal this soft-spoken, blue-eyed athlete.

The Words My Heart Speaks

And the stars in the sky don't shine,
If I can't call you mine.
For my heart you have deeply touched,
And I love you so very much.
And the stars just can't compare,
To just how much I wish I was there.
And the truth I must speak,
For how if you left me, my heart would weep.
And your big smile I can't get enough of,
This feeling I want to call love.
But I'm still just so young,
But from this feeling I won't run.
My heart speaks for itself,
That for my heart there's nobody else.
These feelings and emotions,
Are just too hard to understand.
But I hope you're willing,
To give me a hand.

Tell Me your Story

_____
_____
_____
_____
_____
_____
_____
_____
_____
_____
_____
_____
_____
_____
_____
_____
_____
_____
_____
_____
_____
_____
_____
_____
_____
_____
_____
_____
_____

Sophomore Girl
Feeling Abused

This beautiful girl has proven that it is possible to survive abuse—one day at a time!

My Life

I used to think that life was hard and that it couldn't get any harder.
Little did I know as I got older, the deeper and hotter the water.
First the abuse, from all aspects and angles
To the Lord I cried, asking and searching for help.
Year after year, I cried and I cried,
Living only for my brothers with the little strength left inside.
Finally he's gone, where he belongs locked away,
But I still have nightmares from what happened those days.
Now my brothers are gone too.
Those ignorant people won't let us speak.
I'll find them. I'll see them. They can't stop me.
Now I have my little boy who fills some of that void in my heart.
But deep down inside, there is an empty part.
Now there lies my baby so small and handsome,
I love him so much—even I can hardly fathom.
I cry when I leave in the morning for school.
All day long, it runs through my head to play and sing
To my baby till we nap in my bed.
My heart settles down as I rock him to sleep.
Then I pray and lie down only then to dream.
To dream and to sleep … to wake and to feed him.
To wake up unhappy, content once again.

T
e
l
l

M
e

Y
o
u
r

S
t
o
r
y

Sophomore Boy
Feeling Grief

This very loving boy sat in my chair with his head down as he proceeded to talk about the death of his grandfather, his best friend. One and a half years had gone by since Pop left. The boy was angry and depressed. He was sad that he had never gotten the chance to say good-bye to his grandfather before he died, and he decided to write his good-bye letter to Pop. It turned out that he wrote three letters to Pop before he had the courage to say good-bye. They were written on three consecutive evenings.

Dear Pop,
I know that you are with me forever, and I know that it is hard for me to let you go. I am getting tired of getting upset and depressed all the time. It's very hard for me to say good-bye to you because I never thought that it would come down to this. Now I do not have a father anymore. My real father is somewhere out in the world living his life. When you passed away, it hurt me a lot, but in a way I was happy because you were not in pain anymore. I was so proud of you. My uncle, your son, took a while to get over it. I want to talk to him about how he felt about losing you, but I am too scared. I miss you so much, Dad.

Dear Pop,
Just to let you know that I have your socks. I use those socks to go out to parties or weddings. I do the James Brown just like you. I want to be the man like you were, Pops. Everyone keeps saying that you were the greatest man to meet. I keep saying to myself that if you never had cancer, this family would be just fine. My mother told me that I will have to learn how to control my anger. At the funeral, I did not even cry. I felt that you were sitting right next to me in the place. Right now, I am crying because I miss you so much, Dad. My grandmother keeps saying we will see you again … just wait and see … I hope she is right!

Dear Grandpa,
Pa, I need your help. I've been getting into trouble in school … not doing what they ask me to do. I miss you so much, Pa, that it hurts me. I hope to see you again. One whole week I've been writing to you. I hope you've been reading my letters. Just to let you know, the family is doing really well. We just went to Six Flags last weekend, and we had a lot of fun. I pray to you all the time. I tell God that I want to see you someday, and I know that He will bring you to me. I am trying not to be angry all the time at people who are just trying to say something nice. My mother talks to me about life and the way you are supposed to act. I just wanted to say good-bye to you before you passed away, but I never got a chance to. I miss you so much. We all miss you. You will never be forgotten. I love you always.

Tell Me your Story

The following are excerpts from a very special student's diary (September through June of sophomore year). When she graduated, she gave me gave me permission to share her private thoughts with you. I am forever grateful to her for trusting me! As I read through her diary, I chose several passages that would help you understand her thoughts and feelings. This young girl developed severe anxiety when she was approximately eight years old. The next ten years of her life were engulfed in a roller-coaster ride of ups and downs. She did seek professional help. She chose to stop any medication during her high school years.

Thanks to extremely patient parents and understanding teachers, this beautiful young girl received the support she needed to survive. She was unable to leave any of her classes throughout the day to counsel during school hours, but she sat with me every Friday after school. I found that writing in a diary helped relieve some of her fears. She allowed me to take her diary home during the week and respond through writing. She slowly gained the inner strength she needed to move forward.

She recently arrived at my door with a huge smile on her face. She had just completed her first year of college, and she earned a 3.5 GPA. Anxiety is still a part of her life. She is coping … one day at a time!

9/13

Dear Me,

I was walking home from school and thinking about what to write, in this heart, that I am opening up now. As soon as I got home, I got my clothes ready for the next day. Then I started my Spanish homework, but I was really scared I was doing it wrong, and I was also worrying about my history quiz. Finally, I was able to finish it, and I started reading for the quiz. I could not concentrate at all. My mind was on a horrible clip of a movie I saw in history class about slavery and how they were brought across the Atlantic Ocean.

I stopped, went outside, sat on my doorstep, and read right there. Reading a little section of it and also understanding it really felt good, but the fear of the quiz and getting a bad grade really scared me. I went inside to eat dinner, thinking that's just what I needed. But when I looked at my plate, I wanted to walk back, but I forced myself to eat as much as I could and went back to read.

I finished at ten thirty, and I decided I would refresh my memory in the morning. I set my alarm clock for five o'clock, and then I started to write and think about whether I would be able to sleep or not.

Tell Me your Story

9/19

Today I spent my whole day doing my homework. I always do my homework in the living room, but today I did it in my parents' room. I never felt the strength to do my homework in my own room. I just felt scared, thinking that it will bring back memories. I just sat in their room and did my homework as I timed myself. After I finish it, I'm just going to sit outside and relax.

12/29

Today the whole family was together. We had so much fun; my older cousin completed the Rubik's cube that all my cousins were trying to solve. We talked and played, and my cousins played chess like experts. It was great, but when I left, I felt all my worries coming back. That feeling in my stomach is starting to come back. I'm scared out of my mind.

1/30

My Spanish exam went okay. Right now I have an average of B+. If I did well on my exam, it could bring my grade up (hopefully). Tomorrow I have history and sewing. Sewing, I'm okay with. But history, I really have to study—and I mean study hard. I'm really glad that the worry of next semester is not bothering me too much. I think of it as a new fresh start, and it will be. I will learn new things and meet new people. I shouldn't think of the bad things, and there are no bad things. I will be fine!

1/31

Final exams are over! I hope I did okay on all the exams. I'm trying to stay happy with the new semester. It will be great. I'm going to enjoy this weekend and start out fresh in school. Everything is going to be okay. There is nothing to worry about. I just hope I can keep this confidence on Sunday.

2/1

I am so happy today. A subject that I was so afraid of, I got an A+ (the highest grade on the final). In sewing, I got an A+, but in Spanish, it's really, really bad! I had a B+ average in that class, and I got a B- on my final. Will this average out to a C? Oh, god, this is terrible! And I was thinking of taking Spanish R next year. I'm just so afraid. I don't know what to do—a C on my report card! I knew I was slacking off. I'm going down. I didn't study enough. I don't want a C. I'll take a B- but not a C!

(My response … How about a B+? Look at your report card!)

T
e
l
l

M
e

y
o
u
r

S
t
o
r
y

Today was the best day of my life! I was sitting at home waiting to go to my cousin's house for a get-together. The doorbell rang, and my friend was standing there with a happy birthday balloon. I was so happy. Then my mom and I got ready to go to my cousin's house. When I stepped in the house, it was totally silent. My uncle told me that everyone was downstairs. As I was going, it was pitch-dark. I heard giggling, and all of a sudden, the lights turned on and everyone said, "Surprise!" Oh my god, it was my sweet sixteen surprise party. I was so happy that I almost cried. I had so much fun!

Tell Me your Story

Sophomore Girl
Feeling Insightful

Please enjoy the following questionnaire created by an extremely talented young lady whose vibrant personality undoubtedly makes her one of a kind! It wasn't until her senior year that she allowed me into "her" world. I am ever so thankful that she trusted me enough to share just some of her innermost thoughts.

A few days before graduation, "The Eleven Steps to Overcoming the Overcomeable" were placed on my desk—along with her clever introduction and questionnaire. These words of wisdom were written when she was just sixteen years old—in her sophomore year. Grab a piece of paper and pencil and maybe you will discover something about you!

Mrs. D.

I wrote this about two years ago (if I remember correctly), and upon reading it now (I hadn't read it since it was written), it's pretty clear to me that I wrote it for myself. In those days, I was sure that everyone thought like me. To this day, I sometimes forget that the majority of people don't—heh— but it's still fun to read. Enjoy!

Questionnaire

Date:

Time started:

1. What do you consider to be your worst faults? ("I slack off too often." "I wish to be more open-minded.")
2. Of the faults you have listed, which is your absolute worst (the one that you would like most to change)?
3. Why do you feel that it is such a negative trait? (Give all reasons here—no segregation of emotions here!)
4. What would be the hardest thing for you to accomplish currently with this trait in your way?
5. Is this something you would greatly like to accomplish? Why or why not?
6. Do you honestly wish to change this about yourself? Or do you feel that it is just a part of you that you have lived with thus far and therefore can continue to?
7. Do you honestly think that you can overcome it? Why or why not? (State all fears and doubts here.)

Time finished:

Tell Me Your Story

Eleven Steps to Overcoming the Overcomeable

1. Realize the parts of your personality that you don't always like or want to change. Choose the one part that you like least or want most to change.
   *Upon doing this, you must have good reasons for wanting to change.
   Unacceptable: "My friend says that I need to change this."
   Acceptable: "I feel that it would better my lifestyle and make me a happier person."
   Assigning a level of complexity to your ability of accomplishing certain tasks could prove to be helpful. ("It would be hardest for me to ... but easy to ...")
2. Admit what is wrong about the trait you currently have.
3. You must want to better understand yourself and figure out what makes you act the way you do. Also determine why the negative trait is still in existence and why you want to change it.
   *Denial is not accepted here.
4. Dig deep into your subconscious and clear your mind of all precaution/doubt/denial of your ability to change yourself and your negative aspect.
5. Understand that you are capable of the necessary changes. Take yourself seriously.
6. Dig down even deeper—this time into your consciousness and your self-awareness—and think about why you act the way you do. Notice what makes you who you are so you do not lose your identity in the process of change—and also so that you may get to the root of your negative trait. Think about all of this for a considerable amount of time and examine every aspect of it that you can find.
7. Put together every last thought and find whatever connections may be there.
8. Understand where your problem originated and think about what you can do to overcome it. Sometimes making two lists and comparing them helps greatly. ("The way I feel things should be done" versus "The way I do them.")
9. Start off slowly by practicing the way you know you are capable of doing things, and then gradually make new goals for yourself and increase the complexity level of each goal, referring to the complexity levels assigned to certain tasks for the old you (step 1). Each day you must do something that the old, negative trait you possessed would not let you do. (Starting off small is best!)
10. Replace the negative aspect with a positive one that you can be satisfied with. This may even help you to not judge others as you would have in the past because you have a new outlook on overcoming something negative, and you understand how difficult it can be and how unfortunate others may be for not actually trying to help themselves. Empathy is your best reward.
11. Enjoy your new outlook!

T
e
l
l

M
e

Y
o
u
r

S
t
o
r
y

Sophomore Boy
Feeling Positive

This young boy lit up my office with his optimistic outlook on life from the moment I met him during his freshman year.

My life as a sophomore has been great. So you're probably wondering why and how it is that I feel great. Let me explain. I enjoy school, from its start to end, but I have to admit that many times I don't want to go, since waking up in the morning can be difficult. I am usually very comfortable—my blankets pulled up high to my chin, my head sunk far into my fluffy pillow, and with the warmth of my bed—and this ideal condition can sometimes make waking up a little hard. But I face the fact that I have to go to school, so I get up and begin my day.

Breakfast is very important to me, and I usually eat a bowl of cereal with a glass of ice-cold milk. Breakfast wakes me up and energizes me for the rest of the day. After I wash up and brush my teeth, my mom usually drives me to school since I don't take the bus. Every morning, I get to school a little bit earlier than everyone else because I participate in our school's news production, called PTV. I really like going to PTV, but I'll talk about this a little later with the rest of my activities.

All my classes—Gym, Algebra 2, Chemistry, and English—keep me plenty busy. They are challenging but rewarding. I put a lot of effort into them, and it comes back to me with good grades. All my teachers have totally different personalities, which spices up my day. Their personalities truly fit the subjects they're teaching. For instance, my English teacher is peppy, hip, and very lively, while my laid-back Algebra teacher is serious about teaching the material effectively. Overall, I like my classes, teachers, and classmates. I do get a lot of homework, but I don't mind. Switching classes is the main difference that separates high school from others. It's a time to relax, move about, and spend time with friends. I love it since the hallway atmosphere is pleasant for me.

My high school offers many activities that I am a part of. As mentioned, I am part of PTV, but I am also involved in the ski club, film club, math league, and stage crew. I love PTV, the people who are involved in the production, and what we do. Luckily, my English teacher is the director and throws life into the show. Every morning, the crew of PTV announces events or meetings that will be taking place or have taken place within the various clubs and activities in the school, and we turn this into a news production. I have fun with PTV. I add a little zap into the production, and my friends are especially aware of what I do. I receive mixed reactions from the student body regarding my performances, since I do things a little differently than the other anchors while on camera. I'm very energetic (maybe a little too energetic sometimes) and happy while reading the announcements in front of the fourteen hundred students who are my audience.

Then there is the math league. It's a statewide mathematics competition throughout New Jersey's high schools. There are six tests, each with six questions. If you like hard math questions, come to math league! These questions really get your noggin going, but this is what I love about math league: the challenge is what makes it enjoyable. If you like skiing, the next club I'm involved in is the club for you. Ski club is one of my more relaxing clubs, since I get to spend the night out on the

Tell Me Your Story

mountain skiing with my friends. We go to the Poconos, and the trip is entirely possible through the school. The bus ride can get a little boring sometimes, since the movies usually aren't that great, but it is still fun. Coming home from the trip is just as good, since everyone crashes out and sleeps the entire way back.

I am also involved in the stage crew and the film club. In stage crew, we construct and paint the sets for our school's plays. Our major production that we spent the most work on is the spring play. During construction period on Saturdays, we go to the school and work on the set, which is a lot of fun. Then during the play, the crew is backstage in black clothing, moving the sets during scene changes. For this year's play, I was working the lights, but next year, I very much want to be backstage with the crew moving sets. I can't wait!

The film club can usually be found recording events that happen around our school. From athletic events to award ceremonies, you can be sure the film club will be there, capturing the action. Not to sound conceited, but the director usually asks me to go out into the field and record footage because he thinks I'm good at it. I enjoy all the clubs and extracurricular activities I'm involved in, and I have fun while participating. Another aspect of school that I appreciate is I have a very good reputation with the staff members and the teachers. I'm very polite, respectful, and nice to them, which is probably why I have a good reputation. It is this good reputation that has allowed me to be nominated and receive many awards, such as the Renaissance Award, which is awarded to all-around good students with quality academic achievement.

While at a stage crew meeting, I happened to meet someone. She is a wonderful person who is fun to be around. I enjoy spending time with her. I'm so happy that I've met and gotten to know her better, since she and I connect and get along so very well. This is my girlfriend _____. When I'm not spending time with her or doing schoolwork, I'm relaxing with my buddies. I'm either playing video games or involved in Manhunt. I never have a dull moment. Sometimes we mix it up, and instead of going over each other's houses, we go to a show or the mall—or we just go for a bike ride around town. No matter what we do or where we go, it's always fun.

Religion plays a big part in my life as a sophomore. I'm Roman Catholic and a strong believer in my faith. I turn to my faith for guidance, strength, and comfort. I attend Mass each Sunday with my family and worship. Having faith helps me be a good person and keeps me in line and focused. Without having faith, I don't know what kind of person I would be today. Faith, I can say, has helped shape my life.

Another important aspect of my life is that I am a part of the Boy Scouts of America. I have been involved in scouting since first grade—almost ten years now—and I'm currently active in Troop ____. I'm a life scout and ready to earn Eagle very soon. Eagle is the highest rank in Boy Scouting and is regarded as a very high honor to obtain. Many, many hours of service, leadership, and learning are necessary to earn the rank of Eagle. My journey is nearly complete.

All my merit badges are complete, and I am currently working on my Eagle project. This is a leadership project in which I lead, which is required to earn Eagle. The project is intended to benefit

Tell Me Your Story

the people of my community. My job is to plan, develop, and carry out this project by directing a group of volunteers. The project I plan to do is to improve, beautify, and make safer one of our township's parks. I will be bordering all the playground equipment with plastic borders, filling them in with mulch, planting flower boxes around the park, and improving the park benches and equipment by removing the graffiti and repainting them. Once this project is complete, I can go up for my Eagle Scout Board of Review. This is a meeting where adults from the BSA sit down with me and review my entire scouting career. If I pass, I will have become an Eagle Scout, the highest and most honorable rank in scouting.

Family also plays an important part of my life. Having a solid, stable family, I feel, is necessary to grow and develop in a healthy way. My mom, dad, and brother are always there for me when I need them. They offer me guidance, help, and support. If my family were split, which sadly some families are today, I would not have been able to have that support and nourishment that I am receiving—or have people who are close to me to share my times with. So I am very thankful that I am being brought up in a good environment, which has shaped me to be the person I am today.

I really don't have too many complaints about being a sophomore. I'm content with the activities I'm involved in, the people I'm around, and my personal life. I'm doing pretty well.

T
e
l
l

M
e

y
o
u
r

S
t
o
r
y

Junior Year
Ticket to Freedom!

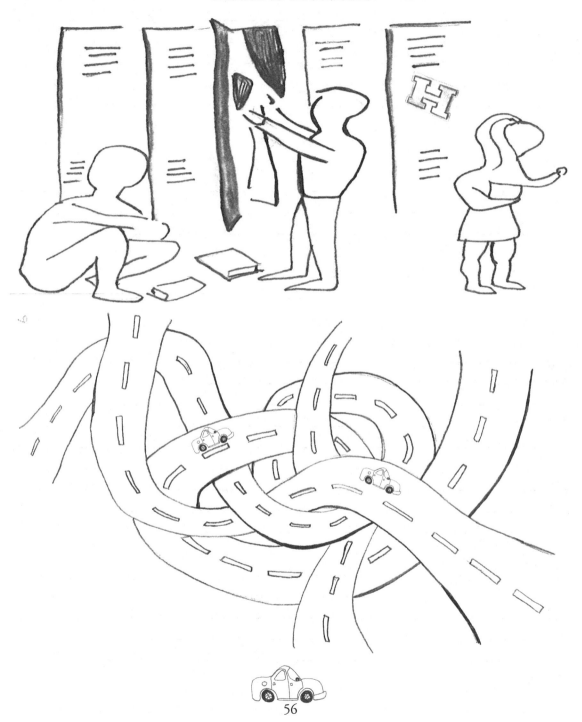

Tell Me Your Story

*Junior Girl
Feeling Sad

This soft-spoken sixteen-year-old rarely came to speak with me. She usually handled all problems on her own, but she needed someone to talk to. If you are feeling sad, please reach out to someone today!

Dear Me,

I know you're having some problems, but I know you'll get through them. You are the strong one in the family, and you'll get through this. I know you miss him a lot and that it makes you cry. But he will be back in a couple of months, and you can talk to him then. I also know that you haven't been in a relationship in a while and that you're afraid to let down your guard a little, but you need to get over it and tell him how you feel.

Who Am I?

I'm a friend. I'm sixteen. I'm smart when I do the work. I'm scared of the future. I get nervous real easily and I become mute. I wake up a million times a night because I think too much. I cry a lot at night. I'm a really depressed teen. I'm a strong student when I'm not distracted. I do a lot for my family and friends. I get mad too easily. I love my family. I am alone. I am sad.

Tell

Me

your

Story

Junior Girl
Feeling Argumentative

A letter appeared on my desk one morning. It was in a sealed envelope accompanied by a school picture. This emotional sixteen-year-old had visited my office for the first time the previous day. She was extremely upset that she and her mother had argued that morning. She couldn't believe how angry her mother had gotten with her. She was devastated. There was no way she could concentrate on schoolwork. I suggested that she phone her mother. There was no answer, but she left a message.

Talking helped her calm down and put things in perspective. She was prepared to speak with her mom as soon as she arrived home from school. Within a few moments, she was able to return to class.

Mrs. D.,

I just wanted to say thank you for talking to me yesterday. You really helped me feel a lot better. I talked to my mom once she got home, and we made up. She was stressed out from work, and that's why she got so angry. I talked to her some more and realized that I was upset about something a close friend said to me. He didn't realize what he had said, but he made me feel unwanted. I talked to him last night, and we made up. He kept telling me how bad he felt because he thought I was joking. We are better though, and I feel so much better. I really appreciate you letting me call my mom—even though I couldn't get through. Also, thank you for giving me some time to cool down. Thank you again.

Love,

T
e
l
l

M
e

Y
o
u
r

S
t
o
r
y

Junior Girl
Feeling Betrayed

This student learned two important life lessons: Life is worth living. Find someone you can trust to talk to.

Dear Me,

Trust is important in life! I don't have one single person in the world. I've lost all trust for friends and family. People lie and betray me. Family takes advantage of trust. To me, a true friend is someone who would do anything in the world for you … someone you can tell anything to … someone who won't tell anyone else … someone who will give advice … someone who will help out however she can … someone who thinks of you before she makes a choice in life that could change or affect you.

I've learned in the past week that I have myself to live for. I have myself to trust and take care of. I haven't made the smartest decisions in the past month, but I don't regret anything—except having trust for anyone! I feel like I have nothing and no one. No one can help me but myself, and I don't know if I want to help myself with anything. I don't want anyone to solve my problems. I want only to trust myself in life. I'm done being afraid to live my life. Life's too short to worry all the time.

People are so ungrateful. I don't mean for this to be a "complaint" about my life. People in this world have it ten times harder. People don't have homes, and people have lost their lives. To me, right now, I'm just causing pain to others, and I am getting in the way. It's not a threat that I want to kill myself. It's saying that I picture life for others as easier without me in it. Trust is hard to find. Never lose trust in yourself!

Tell Me your Story

Junior Girl
Feeling Grateful

This beautiful and intelligent seventeen-year-old is fighting a battle one day at a time. She titled her writing "Hope in the Depths of My Heart."

I am here and I am well and I am grateful. I laugh, and I cannot help but think of a time when laughter and any sort of enjoyment seemed so distant ... when I seemed so distant. I am a young woman of seventeen. I am a five-year sufferer and survivor of anorexia nervosa. I've spent much of the past few years in and out of treatment. Death has tapped upon my door, and though it has been rough, I believe this has only made me stronger. It has shaped much of who I am and what I hold dear.

At first, being hospitalized seems like a death sentence. You are angry and disoriented until you come out. You will not be cured. You will never be cured. But you will become stronger. Your thoughts will become clearer. You will begin to realize that anything short of this intense treatment would have been a death sentence.

I realized that the people I met I will carry with me. We may not all necessarily stay in touch, but they will always remain in my heart. I shared with these strangers what could not be revealed to those most close. At the group meals, we cried in frustration—but we cried together. In group after group, we sat and listened intently. We found comfort in each other. We were all struggling. Consciously or unconsciously, we all made the decision that we were not dying. I know ... every day ... I carry their strength with me.

Tell Me your Story

Junior Boy
Feeling Apologetic

Why is he apologizing for his eating disorder?

Who is _____? He is a lovely young gentleman who has one of the warmest hearts and sweetest personalities you will ever meet in your life. He loves to joke around with his friends and spend quality time with his family where he can really bond with the people who he loves most in the world. But sadly, due to recent troubling choices in his life, those people he loves so much were deeply troubled and worried about the choices he was making. He was eating less than he normally did, and he was eating the wrong types of food that weren't sufficient for the proper growth of a child.

His parents kept telling him to eat—to not be afraid to eat—but he didn't listen. He never thought he would become the type of teenager who thought whatever he did was right and that he knew himself better than others. Looking back, he realizes how idiotic he was, and how foolish he was, especially for not listening to his parents. The changes he was making were taking more of a toll on him than just physically. He was more down and lifeless in his speech. The true self wasn't there. He feels so terrible for putting all his loved ones through this period of sadness and worrying. The people he would do anything for were going crazy worrying about his health and safety while he kept saying, "I'm okay."

But that's all in the past; the true self is here, and he's sticking around. No more crazy diets or anything that will make his true personality go away. Nothing is worth it if it means hurting the people who are the most important in his life. He realizes this now, and he deeply apologizes to anyone he has hurt while going through this.

Tell Me Your Story

Junior Boy
Feeling Spiritual

This boy chose to begin writing just two weeks after his mother's battle with cancer ended. He stopped writing after two months. A year later, he wrote an inspirational college essay, which can be found later in this book.

September _____
Dear Me,

Yesterday was September _____, my mom's birthday. Even though she was not here in the living flesh, I knew she was here in spirit. The previous day, I believed that I would be a crying wreck and couldn't do it. But I woke up, and I felt normal. I woke up and said, "Happy birthday" and then got up from my bed and got ready for school.

My day in school was pretty normal. I got through the day and didn't cry. I went back home and got ready to come back to school for rehearsal. After rehearsal, my father took my brother, his friend, and me—well, my mom too—out to dinner. After we ate, we went home. I stayed up a little bit longer, and then I teared up before I went to sleep. Yet, before I did, I made sure I said, "Happy birthday, Mom!"

October _____
Dear Me,

This weekend was very difficult for me. For most of this weekend, I cried and had great thoughts about my mom's death. I'm a Christian, and I believe that when you die, you go to heaven or hell and you will one day be reunited with your lost ones. I asked myself, "Will I really see my mom again? Should I believe what I'm taught to believe?" I really don't know. I guess there will be a day when I will figure it out. But until that day, I just have to wonder and believe that I will see my mom again one day.

Tell

Me

Your

Story

*Junior Girl
Feeling Frustrated

Why is she ready to explode? Have you ever felt this way?

Dear Me,

I want the money I lent my friend.
Why the heck am I still thinking about him?
I want to get new furniture for my room.
I want to go to that concert in Boston.
I wish my mom could understand what I'm feeling.
Why don't I feel a spark with him?
I'm so darn irritable.
I've been snapping at people.
That stupid druggie in computers won't shut his mouth or take a shower.
Why do guys think it's okay to yell across the room that I'm hot when they have girlfriends?
Why in the world doesn't he think it's wrong to hit a girl?
He better give me that dollar he owes me.
I think I'm getting hives on my face as I'm writing.
My dad picked out a dumb thing to give to my mom from me instead of what I wanted.
I failed like four quizzes, and I'm scared to know what that's doing to my grade.
I wish school started at eight o'clock so I would have more time to get ready because I've been late the past two days.
I gave my last cereal bar to my friend 'cause she was hungry, but I really wanted to eat it next block.
I want to go home and watch my favorite show.
I wish I had his new songs on my phone so I could listen to them when I felt like it.
I wish his CD came out on my birthday instead of waiting till the thirteenth.
I want to have butterflies when I see him, but I don't.

T
e
l
l

M
e

Y
o
u
r

S
t
o
r
y

*Junior Girl
Feeling Numb

Four years had passed since this beautiful young girl was taunted day in and day out by a group of ruthless bullies. Today she comes face-to-face with the leader of the group. Please listen to her powerful and heart-wrenching words.

It was not until one day, my second year of high school, while I was sitting in the counseling office, too anxious to go to class, that I realized that bullies are heartless. The ringleader of the group that bullied me throughout middle school walked into the counseling office, sat down next to me, and proceeded to talk to me as if I were a friend. It took me a while to realize that she had no clue whatsoever that I was one of her victims. She didn't even recognize me or the hurt in my eyes that she saw every day on that bus four years earlier. The humiliation, hurt, and wanting to curl up in a ball and cry all came rushing to me as if I had just been sucked into a black hole and was being hit with all that was buried inside it. After years of therapy and wondering if I would ever return to my old self again—there she was—talking to me as if she hadn't destroyed my life.

I am now a junior in high school and on home instruction because of my anxiety and panic over being in a classroom with teenagers, who, not very long ago, made my life unbearable. I'm not having my story told to everyone for sympathy. I just want school officials to realize that bullying is a serious problem and it is something that needs to be taken care of. Knowing that each school has a system in place to prevent bullying would fill a void in my soul. People who are or were bullied really are victims—the same as someone who lost a leg in a car accident. We didn't lose the ability to walk, but we lost the ability to stand on our own and know that we are important to the world.

If there is anything I could ask for it would be that school officials impose a support group where kids could go to and get support from other teens that went through it or are going through it. It's time to end this "normal part of growing up." It's time to educate people about the harmfulness of bullying before they themselves become part of a group percentage in a statistic.

Tell Me Your Story

Junior Girl
Feeling Angry

This student wrote to her dad seven years after her parents' divorce. Listen to her response to his most recent news.

Dear Dad,

I know that you want to find someone else. You say you are lonely. Well, you have _____, and I always told you we should get another dog! Why did you cheat on Mommy? I know that you were happy. That's one of the few things I do remember. I also know you were drunk when you did it. See, Daddy? That's why I hate alcohol. It makes people do stupid things. What you did was stupid! I hated _____. She was a ——. I hate anyone you introduce me to. They're not my mom and never will be. I won't bond with any of them, and I will *never* call them anything related to Mom.

Mommy is amazing. She's so strong, caring, smart, and fun—the perfect mom. So, why did you do it? You know that's the reason I'm not as close to you as I am to Mom. You were the one at fault. I don't care that our family wasn't and isn't like anyone else's. I care that you hurt her. You were the reason she cried. You were the reason I cried. I never saw Mommy so broken until the divorce. I never saw her cry. It killed me to see her cry. It still does today. Mommy was always a superhero in my eyes. She became human the first time I saw her cry.

I have such a high expectation of guys. It's going to be really hard for me to get a boyfriend because of that. I prefer guys who don't drink or lie. That's going to be really tough to do. I wanna let you know that you acted like a coward tonight. All weekend, while we were with you and for who knows how long, you've been keeping a secret—and I just found out tonight. I doubt you told _____. I'll have to tell him. I was always the one keeping him from harm. Now I gotta save him again so he doesn't find out on the spur of the moment.

I hated the way you told me. You pulled me aside and whispered it to me—and then you just left. You have been dating some woman from work. Let me tell you now so you know: I don't like her. I don't want to meet her. She's not my mother—the one who raised me since birth and knows everything about me and who I can trust. She's just some strange woman—and we're going to meet her this week? Well, if you expect us to eat with her like a family, you're _____ me. I'll be in my room or on the computer all night. I would rather you be gay than with some other woman. I love you, but that doesn't mean that I have to like you right now.

Love,
Me

74

Tell Me Your Story

Junior Girl
Feeling Heartbroken

Breaking up is hard to do!

October

Today is our ten-month anniversary, and he's not in school. He called me yesterday, but I didn't answer my phone. He drove past my house with his friend too. I haven't heard from him since then because he went camping this weekend.

I got a job, but I am not sure if I like it or not. I have my second day of work today from five to ten. And I kind of got over Joe last night. I hung out with one of my ex-boyfriends, and he made me feel good about myself.

Fourteen days later …

It was a crazy weekend. Joe changed a lot. We spent a lot of time together this weekend, and I had a lot of fun. The only problem is that he wants me back—but I am not ready. I am not going to get back with him until he proves himself to me. He's been really nice and sweet to me lately. And he's changed for the better this time. But I am still being careful with him.

Two months later …

Why I love Joe … true love?

Good	Bad
Always there for me	No alone time
Makes me happy	Always with friends
Have a past together	Makes fun of me
Talks about the future	Doesn't call very often
Helps me through problems	Break up all the time
Gives me butterflies	Family doesn't like him
My best friend	No time for friends
Knows when I need a hug	Friends don't like him
Good person to talk to	Sometimes I think I can do better

Six months later …

Joe is finally out of the picture! I have a new boyfriend. He's seventeen and a great person. I know what I had with Joe wasn't happiness. Jeff really makes me happy, and I know that he cares about me. I got a new job too. I work at a deli. It's so much fun, and it pays more than my last job.

T
e
l
l

M
e

Y
o
u
r

S
t
o
r
y

*Junior Boy
Feeling Reflective

This boy is trying very hard to please everyone else—but at whose expense? Is he a regular teenager just growing up? Does everyone his age like to party? Are his risky behaviors causing his anger? Who is he really?

Dear Me,

Who am I? The only person who can ever tell you the answer to that question is one person, and that person is yourself. I am going to tell you who I am. I am a sixteen-year-old high school student who is turning seventeen in about two months. I have a tattoo, and it gives me a lot more self-confidence. I am 100 percent Italian, but I was born in the US. I hate it when people tell me that I'm not 100 percent, because I am. My parents' parents came from Italy, which makes me it—and don't bother telling me that I'm not 100 percent.

I am the kind of kid in school everyone gets along with and everyone knows. I don't have any problems with anyone. I am the kind of person who loves to take risks and enjoy himself and make the best out of any situation. I will do anything to have fun because I love just living life to the fullest. I don't want to look back on life and think, *Why didn't I do that?*

I don't ever want to grow up. I always want to be a kid, and I know I will. I don't want to get older and get mature and just be strict and hate everyone and everything. I'm going to be that eighty-year-old grandpa tripping people with my cane and hitting them with it. Even though I am young, I like to go out and party. And, yes, everyone at my age does that. But I actually have fun and make everyone else have fun.

I love to just hang out and relax and party with friends and get away from the reality that surrounds me. I love to drink, and I have smoked pot sometimes. I stopped because I get paranoid. I don't get like that now, but I do it every now and then just like everyone else does. I am the type of kid who will try anything new. I am the type of kid who is a jokester and does not take anything too seriously. I always joke around and make people laugh, and I don't care what other people think most of the time.

In and out of school, I constantly mess around and entertain myself along with others. I hate school and despise it, but it's something I have to go through no matter what. I love blonde girls and brunette girls, but they need good personalities to go with their good looks. Otherwise, I don't bother. I think girls with tattoos are very attractive, and I don't really know why.

I am an outgoing, down-to-earth person. I can sit and hang out with you no matter what age you are, and I guess that's why I get along with most people. I will also do anything for you if you are a good friend. My friends mean the world to me; without friends, you would have nothing to do all day. I have a lot of friends, but I only hang out with certain ones every day. There are about eight of us. Sometimes I hang out with other people just to get away from the same things I do every day.

T

e

l

l

M

e

Y

o

u

r

S

t

o

r

y

Along with all this comes a downside that I don't show most of the time. Lately, I cannot hold it in anymore. I get so angry that it's hard for me to hold back. I can't really control myself. I can get mad real fast. When I get like this, I can't deal with people; if you look at me, I'll get even angrier. After this is over, I will be very quiet and want to have nothing to do with anyone. I just want to be left alone. I also will be the first one to tell a joke and make fun of someone and get made fun of back and laugh along. But when people just keep going, I get really angry and hate it. I'm pretty sure those are the only bad things to me, which aren't too bad. I just have a very bad temper, which can be the downfall of me. I have to learn to control it. All in all, I am just a regular teenager who is growing into the person I am going to be for the rest of my life—and I am ready.

Tell Me Your Story

*Junior Girl
Feeling Guilty, Helpless, Lonely, Rejected, and Confused

One night can change your life!

Dear Me,

It was a warm August day, yet it felt so dark and cold that night. It started out that my two best friends and I were going to _____'s party. I had to lie to my mom, which was mistake number one. I was up in my room getting ready to "sleep over" at my friend's house. I was wearing old shorts and an old T-shirt.

When I looked out my window, I knew this whole party thing was a bad idea. I saw a cardinal fly across the woods in the back of my house. There was a story behind the bird. My mom's mom said that when she died, she wanted to come back as a red cardinal. It hit me right then and there that it was wrong, but I decided to still go, which was mistake number two.

I went to my girlfriend's house, changed into better clothes, and went to the party. We got there and were having a good time with a bunch of our best friends, but I guess I didn't know my limits. I started slurring my words, and the rest was history. I really don't know what happened at that party, but from what my best friend said, I was making a big fool out of myself. I was yelling and screaming. She said I passed out for about a half hour, woke up, and went crazy again. Then I started getting hysterical. This part … I remember. I was screaming, "Take me home! Take me home! I want my mom! She'll understand." I finally was taken home by a girl who had graduated the year before. Thank God for her! I got home, not knowing what to expect. My mom took care of me the best she could, and I love her so much.

The morning after was total hell. I was woken up at eight in the morning by my noisy pool filter. I looked out that same window I had the day before and felt like a complete a———. From then on, I was hated by mostly all my old friends, except for one. But my old friends, the ones who I grew up with, hated my guts and wanted to kill me. I felt helpless and unwanted by everyone. I can't even go to the movies without them all being there saying, "Go home, b———." I hate it … and I hate them. But what I don't understand is ____'s parents. They found out about the party and know what he and his friends did, yet his parents still let him hang out with them and get drunk all the time! I just don't get it!

Six months have now passed, and I still feel like I can't be anywhere they are—or else I have an anxiety attack. I feel like I am unwanted. For some odd reason, I want to be accepted by these people who have put me through hell. I want to do something about this, but I'm scared they won't let me even sit at the same lunch table. I just hate feeling rejected. It was a stupid mistake I made that night, and if I could go back and do it all over again and not go, I would so go back!

These people have made fun of me and made my life hell. Whenever I'm in the same room, they make comments and throw-up noises. I hate it. This only happens when it's ____ and all his friends. If it were just the two of us, he would walk the other way. You see, last year he used to like

Tell Me your Story

me. I think that has something to do with it. ____ would never do anything physical because of my boyfriend. ____ plays football with all of them and is friends with all of them and doesn't care what they say about me. I don't hang out with many people anymore except for ____ and my six best girlfriends. For me, that's enough. I'm not a drinker, and that wasn't me.

I'm a good kid who has values, gets good grades, loves her parents, and loves her life. That August night, I was a different girl—and I hate it. And I hate all those boys. Whenever they are brought up in a conversation, I have to pretend like I don't hear it. Whenever I hear any of their names, it's like I feel uncomfortable, but I guess in this kind of situation, it's normal. I just need help getting though this because I'm very stressed. I want your help, Mrs. D., please.

T
e
l
l

M
e

y
o
u
r

S
t
o
r
y

Junior Girl
Feeling Inadequate

Two years went by before this funny, intelligent, blue-eyed blonde decided to trust me.

Dear Me,

Who am I? That's a question I've been trying to answer for sixteen years now. I still don't really know how to fully and honestly answer this, but I will try. Let's start with what everyone knows. I am a sixteen-year-old high school junior who gets pretty much straight A's, has a torturous older brother, and has frequent "blonde moments." I dance. I am deathly terrified of clowns (and that's an understatement). Oh, and I absolutely love and always will love 'N Sync!

Now what few people know about me. I have the most dysfunctional family there is! You see, my family (now get ready for this) consists of depressed and bipolar people, manipulators and liars, racists, prostitutes, and an excessive amount of alcoholics and drug addicts. I am so proud to say that neither I nor my immediate family are anything like these fools. I refuse to be anything like these people! I will never sell myself. I will never lose all my possessions and family because they were trying to help. I am quite ashamed that this has to be my background, my blood, but it is. I suppose this is for a reason though, right?

Now for what no one really knows about me or who I am. I am not very trusting at all. Although I may know you are a good person who wants to help, I will not open up to you or let you into my life. This is most likely because of my family. They were supposed to be there for me. They went and stabbed me in the back, and I completely lost all my trust and respect for them. They made me put up my guard. Another thing is I push people away. This is something I recently realized. Every time somebody gets too close to me, I start to finally let them in—and then I do something to make them leave completely or take a few steps back. I hate myself for doing that because I want to let them in. I want to trust them, but I can't. I think that when I get too close to someone, they are just going to break my heart, stab me in the back, or leave. I don't want that to happen—again.

Lastly, I am a girl who feels like she is inadequate—whether it is letting a friend down, not being a better dancer, or not living up to my mother's expectations. Even though I get straight A's, I feel like it is never good enough for my mother. This especially becomes evident when my brother enters the picture. Everything he does is fabulous, excellent, and outstanding. He is a great athlete (woo hoo!). He gets two or three C's on his report card—or even a D or an F—and he's still the golden child. What the h——?

Overall, we teens are all the same. We are all just trying to survive in this crazy world. We are all trying to impress someone. We are all trying to fit in, and we are all trying to find a way to accept ourselves for who we are or fix what is wrong. We all come with our own personal experiences. I am a blonde 'N Sync-er who babysits. I have an insane family. I can't trust anyone. I can't let anyone in because too many people have broken that trust. I am me!

Me

Tell
Me
your
Story

*Junior Girl
Feeling Controlled

This very smart sixteen-year-old originally told me that she transferred schools to get away from friends who were harassing her. Who was she really running away from?

Dear Me,

It's been a while since I've actually confronted my feelings. I miss the old me, and I just want to get back to the way things used to be. No more hurt, crying, fake smiling, or just wanting to die. Sometimes I think, *Why don't I just give up?* But then I realize that what hurts me only makes me stronger.

The people who have hurt me would love to see me break down and lose it. But I've got to keep myself sane. I often feel so little—like I've been crushed and smashed into millions of pieces that no one can ever fix. And I now realize it's not the way out, regardless of the situation I'm in. Physical pain only brings more emotional pain. More emotional pain, I've learned, leads to more physical pain. The process repeated itself until I realized I didn't want to hurt anymore. I didn't want to walk around with fake smiles. I didn't want to forget what a genuine laugh felt like. And I didn't want to lose myself anymore than I already had.

I was scared and alone when all my problems started. I didn't know who, if anyone, I could confide in because all the trust I put into my friends was just thrown in a shredder. After a little less than a year had passed, I knew it was time for all my hurt and troubles to cease. I wanted so bad just to be happy again, and luckily I'm on the right track now. Someone who I recently met told me, "Everything will be all right." And for once, I believe that person with everything I have.

Me

Five months later ...

Today this beautiful young girl arrived at my door with a great big smile! She just finished a five-day stay in the hospital for drugs. Her face was glowing, and her eyes were gleaming! "I'm twelve days clean!" In her voice, there was life. There was strength. There was hope. She was alive!

You see, she admitted to using drugs about two weeks prior to her hospitalization. She came to my office, desperate and crying. She said, "I have to tell the truth. I can't lie anymore. I'm using drugs. I hate myself. I want to stop."

She was tired of living in the world of darkness. She was ready for help. Within an hour, she faced her worst nightmare: telling her mother about her drug use! I asked her if she would continue writing her story. She said, "Yes." So, I am going to stop now and wait for her to write.

Just a few weeks passed by, and she quickly lost all control of her life. Drugs controlled her life. She found herself in legal trouble for destroying property. She ran away for five days and was found by the police. She spent three nights in juvenile detention, and she was put on house arrest. She

T

e

l

l

M

e

y

o

u

r

S

t

o

r

y

changed schools. She stopped using. She had no contact with her friends. She continued counseling. She was given a second chance.

Three months later ...

Dear Me,

It's been a while, and I have more fear than ever. Boy, did I fall—and it slapped me in the face hard. So, I'm on the rising, doing day-by-day—or minute-by-minute—living. Apologies mean nothing more than dirt when they're not sincere; they're just like unfulfilled promises. I'm trying to become a new me—in a positive way this time. I know it's going to be a journey, but I'm used to them. I'm scared this time because I have no footsteps to follow. It's me in this path, looking back on my own steps and wondering when the journey will be smooth.

Everything is on my shoulders. I need that pressure. I could just cry rivers—or oceans—because I let so many people down. What was I thinking? Drugs controlled the hell out of me. Looking back, I hate that person. I feel like I was living on another planet and suddenly came down to earth. Things are so different. I really believe in God now. I used to think it was all His fault, but I was so wrong. When I'm really low, I pray to Him or actually think in my head and give it time. He brings me back up—even when I think things will never look up.

This walk is a process. I took a wrong turn, and now I'm on the "uphill." Time is all it takes. Once again, everything's going to be all right. That's a promise I will fulfill: to prove my old self wrong!

Signed,
The girl who now chooses to know right from wrong

T
e
l
l

M
e

y
o
u
r

S
t
o
r
y

Junior Girl
Feeling Sad

Yesterday I was asked to recommend a student from the junior class who has made the most progress since freshman year. I didn't have to think too much. I had just had a conversation with one of my junior girls whose life mimicked many students in high school. She and I were reviewing her final transcripts when her freshman year ended. She had the opportunity to earn forty credits, but she only earned ten credits. Graduation wasn't looking too good.

We talked about her choices and goals—and the fact that she still had time to get on the right track. There was hope. She could graduate with her class. The next day, she came in to me and said, "I screwed up. I'm not going to do it again. You will see."

Two years later, she followed through with the commitment to herself, and she has continued to pass every course she has taken. As of today, she will be graduating with her senior class! She now helps me counsel students who need a wake-up call. She is my motivational mediator and is the leader of our group, which is known as the M&M group! The following writings were written during her junior year and senior year.

Dear Me,

I wish I didn't have to pretend to be happy. I wish I naturally were. Today, so far, is a good day, but I fear that when I return to reality, I'll no longer smile. I am tired of hearing about how I should be more responsible. I can't put up with the pressure or the emotional put-downs. I try and try, but nobody sees or realizes how much pressure there is and when to back off.

12:19 a.m.

Dear Me,

Why are you so sad today? Why are you always sad? You have a lot of people who love and care for you. Although things are tough, it doesn't mean things can't get better. I know you're feeling like all four walls are closing in on you … like you're screaming and nobody hears you. It's like you're falling, and once you lose your balance, you need to hit rock bottom before you can get back up.

You seem to be a tower of strength that occasionally falls. What you need is to get yourself situated and learn to keep it that way. This is difficult. I won't lie. I think you may need to see a counselor outside of school. If that doesn't work, find new surroundings for yourself. Just remember everything passes. Sometimes it takes a while, but everything eventually passes. Faith, patience, and hope will help you get by.

Love always,
Me

Tell Me your Story

12:58 a.m.

Dear Me,

I understand life is hard, but why does it have to be *this* hard? After my amazing summer, I knew things would be hard when school started. The feeling in my stomach alone warned me that things would get rocky. I just didn't know the extent of how rough.

For starters, my mother and sister got into trouble while I was six thousand miles away—having the time of my life with the boy I love. I sat at the airport for six hours by myself, and I heard the news of their arrest. For the entire trip home, I did nothing but cry—during all three flights. The fact that I was leaving to come back home alone was upsetting enough. However, knowing what I was coming home to was even more devastating.

Then came my mother's habits and discovering that my mom had stolen money from my family. Her habit—or should I say addiction—completely took over her. At that point, only a rehabilitation center could save her. Oh, and on top of all this, DYFS was hounding us to get tested for drugs. Now, she voluntarily signed herself into rehab, which is a great thing. However, it is very difficult to handle. As I speak, my grandma is taking care of me by living here. This has been a huge adjustment. For years, I have been taking care of myself and was able to do whatever I wanted. Now, it sometimes feels like I am under a constant surveillance. Don't get me wrong: I love my grandma, but this dramatic change makes me feel smothered. I know it's only because she loves me.

Also, the one thing that has just recently started to bother me is _____. My friend has broken his heart over and over again, leaving me to pick up the pieces. During all of this, I became attracted to him. Then I began developing feelings toward him. Now I don't know what to do. Those who see it and know say, "Go for it. You look so cute together." How do I get him to stop liking her? How do I get him to open his eyes to see what is right in front of him? Me!

Yes, of course I still love _____, but I have called it quits for right now due to the previous circumstances. And frankly, I see us being just good friends in the end. On top of all this, I am practicing sobriety. Not only for myself, but to set a good example for my mother when she comes home. I am the one who has to be strong for her in order for her to pull through this. Someone, please help me!

Love always,
Me

Tell Me your Story

95

Junior Girl
Feeling Ordinary

She likes to make everybody else smile. Why—and at whose expense?

Dear Me,

Turn around. See that random girl who practically blends into the background? Absolutely ordinary in every way. She doesn't stand out, unless it's gym class because then she's playing football—and she's a beast. Hello, who are you? That's me. I've never been good at describing myself. Words will come, but I'm afraid to be wrong. I'm not even sure you can be wrong at those things, and I'm still scared about it, especially when we have to do personality surveys. I play hockey, softball, and football, but I'll ask someone who "knows" me if it's okay if I write athletic. At first, I couldn't figure out why I should write this. Actually, I was taken back. I've never had to overcome a personal struggle that could go up against the difficulties so many are facing. I haven't had a baby in high school or tried to kill myself, and I've been drug-free since the day I popped out. So why me? I'm not sure either.

The place I call home is crawling with kids, and I'm related to most of them. Being a junior, I am the oldest of five. My house is crazy, and the five of us only love one another secretly. I think some of the physical fights we've had are worthy of the Coliseum. I'm not crawling with friends, but I love the ones who, for some reason, stuck around. Their personalities range, and they are so individual. They're all going somewhere. I wonder if they will leave me in their dust? I think I feed off of them in an effort to take the qualities I admire and paste them to myself.

Most people are afraid of physical things like spiders and clowns, but me? Not so much. They actually call me the brave one. In the city once, two of my very good friends and I needed to go up these stairs. It was pitch-black, and the staircase had open doorways that were equally as dark. They were kind of scared, but they wanted to see the store at the top. I went first, even checking out the doorways. I wouldn't have let them go first anyhow. If something bad would have happened, I'd rather it happen to me because I wouldn't be able to look at myself if I let that happen. Oh yeah, I guess that makes me brave.

Honestly, I'm not brave at all. I'm scared of things that you feel. I'm scared to be wrong. I'm terrified to death that I'll never amount to much and that I'm not good enough to deserve my wonderful friends. I notice all my flaws, and nothing I do is ever good enough for me. I set standards so high for myself; there is no one alive who could reach them. I beat myself up when I fall short.

I'm afraid I'm dispensable and easily replaced. I have trouble with feelings. I don't like to bother people with my troubles; instead, I soak it all up and don't let it out. Then I grab my Elmer's glue stick and plaster on my smile. I don't want to be a burden, and I want to be worth your while. I can't cry. I guess that makes me seem cruel. If you don't know me, I think that's how I'd come across. I'm extremely polite. I'll respect you and be nice to you, but don't you dare do anything to my friends—as some people have found out. I'm a force to be reckoned with, and I can get up from any hit.

Tell Me your Story

You could tell me the worst news ever, and I'd just take it. You'll never see me cry. I only do it when I'm alone. I can't accept compliments. If you tell me I look nice, I'll just laugh and ask how you're feeling. I won't believe you. I'm trying to work on that one though. My best friend takes pride in the fact that she's seen me cry. I guess she's happy to see something about me that no one else has seen since I was like five and got teased for my velcro *Mulan* shoes. If they'd fit, I'd still wear them. I've been dragged by a dog, hit in the face by a rock, and needed stitches in my tongue. (I didn't think they gave stitches there either, but I got about twenty from a slap shot in hockey.) I didn't cry and I don't think that my eyes even teared up. I think I'm scared to be weak. When something's wrong, my sisters usually come to me. If they're crying, how can I blubber too? That's inconsiderate of me, I think. I guess I come across as a tough guy because it's kind of like I fall somehow. Does that make sense? Wow, look how brave I am now.

Among my many faults is my sarcastic mouth and always needing to get in the last word. It's a problem that makes me difficult if you don't know me. It gets me into trouble and has ruined many moments, moments I desperately want back so I can fix them. I don't think I'd be friends with me. I really cannot comprehend how I have any.

Another of my many faults is I do things for other people. I always put others before myself, and anything anyone wants always comes before what I want. I don't really know what I'm doing for me and what I'm doing so someone else will smile—even if it's at my own expense. I'm working on that too.

I always play back recent conversations and go over what would have been better to say instead of what I actually said. I'm such a dork. I'm confused, I'm scared, and I'm not crazy about me. I think I'm supposed to explain how I survive. Well, what keeps me walking and breathing? I guess it's the little things: the occasional letter in the mail and those perfect moments where everything clicks. I love when it's raining and you drive under a bridge and the rain stops and then starts again. I love colors, and I love hitting a home run. I love making you smile. I think you need to have death and sadness to truly appreciate a smile and life. I think that's why I get up in the morning.

Does this scatterbrained, messy note to myself make sense? Live for the little things that make you smile—whatever they may be. I guess those are my words of wisdom. Ha, I'd never thought I'd have those. That should make you know yourself better. I'm still working on it, but I guess you could say I'm getting there.

Tell Me Your Story

Junior Girl
Feeling Pensive

This sixteen-year-old writes to herself, and sometimes she writes to the love of her life. She titles her journal entries to him "The Jimmy Chronicles," but she never allows him to see what she has written.

Dear Me,

It's 10:40 p.m., and you're still writing this. You feel like if you don't get it all out, you're gonna explode, right? Well, go ahead, but don't blame me if you fall asleep in school tomorrow. So what first? Boys? That sounds like a good enough place to start since they are always on your mind. To get it right out in the open, you are the biggest hopeless romantic I've ever met. You've watched so many movies and read so many books that your expectations are really high. You've even got a list of qualities you want in a guy, but we're not going into that—or we'll be up all night.

I know what's been bugging you—no matter how many times you deny it. You know it's true. It's Jimmy. Ever since you met him, he hasn't been very far from your mind. Then when he just dropped you, you couldn't take it. You thought he was perfect and different from the guys you liked in the past, and for a while, he was. But once you went on vacation, everything changed. I know you blame that vacation. You miss Jimmy and the way he treated you, like you were the only thing that mattered. So you denied it, to not seem obsessive, but you are.

You are really obsessive, OCD to the max, but you tried to find someone else and you did. You found _____. The thing is that you're still not sure about him. You know he's a great guy and that you like what you've seen and heard, but there's a chance that he might not like you. It seems that he does at times, but you're not so sure at other times. Today, in gym, you could have sworn that he held your hand a bit longer than was necessary for the activity. You have a lot of guy friends and like the attention you get from them. It makes you feel special. So since we've spent more than a page discussing boys, let's get to friends.

You love your friends because you never had the sister you wanted. You'd die for them, to make it simple. Like tonight, you took over a friend's shift at work so _____ wasn't alone. It caused you to stay up till twelve thirty to finish chemistry. You never finished your algebra, but you can do that at lunch. But you know a friend has changed, and you don't like it. You tell yourself it's for her own good, but you know better. You know it's because you were always the self-confident one who got all the attention, the leader of your friends, I guess. Anyway, people always went to you, and you were the one boys looked at. Now she feels better about herself because she's decided to act like her sister. Her sister is just like you, but different in a sense. But you always want to be the leader, and now you feel you're not. Okay, so you're a control freak. A big one, I might add. You just have to learn to accept that and the fact that you can't change her. It may be hard, but in the end, it will be worth it.

Let's talk about the way you strive to please people. When you told Mom that you were taking a friend's shift tonight, she was so proud. You couldn't bear to tell her that you would be up all night doing homework. You just want her to be proud of you, and even though you know she already is,

Tell Me your Story

you still strive to be the perfect child most of the time—except when you fight. You hate fighting with Mom. She's your confidante, best friend, teacher, and so many other things. You would be so lost without her. You stayed up late doing chemistry so you would get a good grade and make her proud. But you have to stop staying up so late. You know it's beginning to wear you down. On Tuesday, you just broke down and couldn't take it anymore.

Stop thinking about everything. That's what this letter is for, right? To get all your thoughts out? But your imagination is so active you're going to think of something sooner or later. It doesn't take much for your mind to come up with something to make it hard to sleep, and it's always stuff you wonder about, that you never know the answer to. What if you had done one thing differently today? Would that have changed your entire day? Would you be sleeping now? Who knows? You don't, but you want to know.

You have so many questions that you always think about before bed—and that's what keeps you up. Well, I forbid you to think about them or write about them anymore. Go to sleep! Trust me—you'll thank me in the morning. (1:21 a.m.)

Love,
Me

Dear Jimmy,

I'm so helplessly stuck on you. I hate being obsessive like this. I told you about these letters. I don't know what made me do it. I just told you, and you want to read them. That's odd enough. My friends saw you on Saturday. I didn't, so I called you. That was my second mistake. My first was falling for you and your bull. So, anyway, I'm not sure what I was expecting: a declaration of love? Yeah, something like that. Well, you were so nice to me—so nice—and I would rather you weren't. I would rather have you yelling at me or mad at me or something. Anything so I could hate you.

You said there were some things you would change if you could go back. In relation to me or us, I guess. Yeah, well you screwed up royally and screwed me over. Oh, but that's right, you didn't screw me. You screwed her! I don't like hating someone I don't know, but you got me doing it. In the words of Kevin Lyttle: "You get me going crazy." I wanted to dance with you to that song so badly. I still want to dance with you because I never got to. I don't know if I'm going to show you these. Who knows? Maybe you'll see them on the shelf at Barnes and Noble one day. Now maybe I can sleep. I still "think" I love you. Hence, I still don't know what love is … too young … but one day I will. It won't be you—I promise. For now, you can have the pleasure of knowing you were my first high school love.

Love,
Me

Tell Me your Story

Dear Jimmy,

I was sad to hear that you and _____ broke up. What? Ha ha. No, I wasn't—more like really happy. Yeah, that's it. So, anyways, what's the reason you guys broke up? You asked her to stop drinking and smoking pot. She couldn't do it and didn't want to, so she broke up with you. Oh, how the mighty have fallen! I talked to you, and you said you wanted a girlfriend. I said wait a bit so you can get over her and not have a rebound girl. You weren't sure. But you do know I listen to you. I remembered you hate girls who drink. Well, if she drinks, then she's not right for you. I still want to go to cotillion with you. Who knows? Maybe I'll be over you by then … maybe not. Anyways, I'll sleep easy tonight.

Love,
Me

Tell Me Your Story

Senior Year
Ready for Takeoff!

T
e
l
l

M
e

y
o
u
r

S
t
o
r
y

Would being around her really end his problems?

Dear Me,

I have no clue how to overcome the problems I am having right now between so-called friends and all the other s——— like drugs and not using them. Let's put it this way: I am going nuts over it all. I also am having problems with the girl in my life. She is extremely worried about me and what is going on right now. If only I were around her the whole time, I wouldn't have these problems. She keeps me calm and out of trouble. I also have to stay away from some of my so-called friends and many others. But it's not easy when you don't like to be lonely and without anyone to talk to. She wants to be friends right now, and that is what I really need: a true friend who won't abandon me when things get hard or out of control.

Tell

Me

your

Story

Senior Girl
Feeling Curious

The following note was left on my desk by an extremely intelligent and creative seventeen-year-old. Her high school years were filled with self-doubt and low self-esteem. She was unable to see the beautiful person she truly was. (By the way, her curiosity did not get the best of her. She decided not to use!)

Mrs. D.,

I'm only gonna do it 'cause I'm curious. I know it's illegal. I know it can give me a weird or horrible effect, but I won't know unless I try it. Drugs are drugs—they're just there. If it hits me the wrong way, I know I won't ever do it again, provided I am still alive. But I won't be okay unless I try it and know how it feels. I believe that I need to try something outrageous that you and I know I wouldn't normally do under the circumstances. However, I'm not saying that if there's an opportunity to try other drugs, I'll jump on the bandwagon and try them. Actually, I'll do the opposite and turn away. I just feel that I need to try this.

Me

Tell Me Your Story

Feeling Lonely

This extremely mature seventeen-year-old wrote a letter to her father who had passed away when she was eleven. His death created a world of confusion for this vulnerable girl. Throughout high school, she was a part of our bereavement group for those who had lost parents or guardians. Initially, she chose not speak. By senior year, she helped me run the group! If you are grieving a loss, please get help. You do not have to go through this difficult time alone.

Dear Daddy,

I just want you to know that waking up each morning knowing that you're not going to be here has become very difficult for me. But you know what? Every morning I wake up for you because I know I can't give up—and I know you won't let me. I just want to be a good person and for you to be proud of me. I'm so jealous of my friends who have fathers because they'll have the chance to walk their daughters down the aisle or kiss them good night or just say, "I love you." But every night when I go to sleep, I know you're there smiling down on me. I know that you will always be there when I need you. There is so much I want to say to you, to tell you, but all I can think of right now is "I love you, and I miss you so much."

Love always,

Tell Me Your Story

Senior Girl
Feeling Reflective

What a great synopsis of four years in high school!

Dear Me,

With the school year coming to an end and graduation right around the corner, I sit here in total amazement. It's hard to grasp the concept that my high school career will soon be over. It feels like it was just yesterday that I was a shy, scared, fourteen-year-old girl walking through the halls of this enormous high school as a freshman.

I am writing this as a scared eighteen-year-old young woman who is ready to embark on her journey out into the real world. There isn't one single word that can sum up four years of experiences, memories, and many, many lessons learned. It's impossible! It's kind of like one big roller coaster: the ups, the downs, the loop de loops. Making new friends, getting your license, going to the prom, getting involved in extracurricular activities … the list goes on and on.

It's not all fun and games though. SATs, friendships that you thought would last a lifetime, growing apart, fights, and tears too. I believe that through everything, the most important thing that I've learned is something that I'll carry with me in life: In every decision that you make, there's a lesson that follows. It's up to you to learn from it and move on with the knowledge you've gained. It's all one big test for the real world.

As my ride is quickly coming to an end, I look back on all that I've accomplished. I can't help but smile. I hope that everyone who's just getting on the high school roller coaster will truly make the best out of his or her four years and come out in the end a mature, responsible young adult with memories that'll last a lifetime—just like I did!

T
e
l
l

M
e

Y
o
u
r

S
t
o
r
y

This beautiful, soft-spoken, blue-eyed girl begins to trust and reaches out for help.

Dear Me,

I am a sixteen-year-old, abused, lost, hurt, friendless, friendly, uncomfortable, homeless, helpless, scared, trapped, hateful, loving, careless, honest, best secret keeper, accidentally in the middle, crazy, party animal, easy to love, clean, trustful, sensitive, helpful, intelligent, fighter, runaway, strong, reader, writer, inventor, great listener, great speaker, joker, Beatle lover, melancholy, naughty and nice, hero, poor, and in pain.

I am all of those things and maybe more. I fought six battles with my dad, lost three friends and one boyfriend, and lost my home three times. My cousin hates me because of my other cousins. I am the definition of the quote "People don't see what they don't want to see."

I lost all my pets: two cats, two rabbits, two guinea pigs, and three pugs. I saw three of my cats die. I am not afraid of death, but I am not willing to take mine. I love my mom a little too much, and I hate my dad's actions toward me and how he doesn't help.

I am losing my own battle at life. These obstacles have me tied up, and I'm having trouble getting out. I feel uncomfortable, and I need help coping at school. I miss everything in and about my old school. I don't understand God's actions and the reasons why this is happening. I have seen more than my peers, and I need a secret keeper and trustworthy person to tell everything to.

Tell Me your Story

Senior Boy
Feeling Lost

This boy speaks of his father's death and its impact on his life as a chapter for his senior memory book.

Before I was, there was …

While I was growing up, my family was always around. They were loud and annoying most of the time, but they're still my family, no matter what. The only two people who really paved the way for me—well, three people, actually—were my mom, my dad, and myself. My mom and dad are two completely opposite people, and that's what started the molding for me. The rest was—and still is—up to me. I had a good childhood when I was growing up. My parents were divorced, but I saw my dad so much that it was like he was always there with me. I loved it. No, my father isn't around anymore. He died when I was in eighth grade, the first day of school. Ever since then, the person I was has been long gone—and I don't think he's ever coming back.

When my dad died, I died. I can't even remember how I acted when I was growing up. It's like I took who I was at that time and just crushed him down so deep inside me that I lost him forever. I was forced to make someone new out of what I had left. I became, I guess one could say, antisocial. I started keeping to myself, rarely talking to anyone for more than five minutes. I also started learning things on my own.

Most kids growing up have their parents. I had just my mom. She did her best trying to make up for my dad not being there—and I know she tried, and still is, trying her best, and I love her like no tomorrow for it. Even though I don't show it as much as I should, she knows I do. The person I created for myself has consumed me. It's like a virus. It's always going to be there, dwelling inside me, never to leave me.

It scares me that I'm never going to know who I would have been if my father had not died. In a way, I've gotten used to this being who I am. Maybe I was destined to be this way and all this searching I've been doing trying to find what was lost has been inside me all this while. If that's true, I've just yet to find it. Or … maybe … I know it's there, and I don't want to find it. Because knowing I found it means I'll have to let go.

Tell Me your Story

*Senior Girl
Feeling Hopeful

For the past five years, this letter has been tucked away for safekeeping in her parents' safety deposit box. That is how much of an impact these words made on her mother and father. When this tearful young girl wrote this letter at my desk, I walked out of the room to give her the privacy she needed. I remember that day clearly, and I am thrilled that her letter has made its way into my book! She went to the college of her dreams and recently graduated with honors!

Dear Mom and Dad,

I am writing this letter to tell you exactly how I feel. Every time we try to talk about college, it always ends up being a fight. So I thought this would be much calmer. I understand that money is a major factor in deciding what college I will be going to, and I am sick of fighting over it. I just want to let you know where I am coming from. You know that I love both of you to death, but I also want to feel independent. I really want to go to _____, and you know that, but I am willing to go look at _____ with you on Saturday. I just feel that I deserve to go away to a college that I know I will enjoy.

I feel that I have accomplished a lot in my life already. I have always worked hard in school, and I am never in trouble. I am a leader, and I don't follow all the others who are into drugs and alcohol. I have learned my lesson and learned from my mistake. I came out in the top 10 percent of my class, and I have never gotten a grade lower than a B. I am very involved in sports and other activities. I am always busy. I stay out of trouble, and I am not a bad daughter. I am not trying to suck up to you. I am just trying to prove that I deserve everything that I can get.

I don't understand how you used to pay for _____ to go to college. Wasn't that a lot of money too? Now he is only going to the county college. I really want to go to _____, and I am willing to take on the responsibility of paying off a loan. I am sick of fighting over this. I just wanted you to know that I am trying.

I love you …

T

e

l

l

M

e

Y

o

u

r

S

t

o

r

y

*Senior Boy
Feeling Distraught

This young man arrived in my office on a sunny spring day. He couldn't stop crying. As he spoke, I felt the depth of his sadness. His parents and the child-study team were notified immediately. Within moments, his parents listened to his tearful words and promised to get him the help he needed. The secret that was tearing him to shreds was his sexuality. He was not ready to tell them. About two weeks later, he had the courage to tell his parents that he was gay. Their response is what every child who is in the midst of such turmoil hopes for. They let him know that they will always love him and accept him for who he is.

Dear Me,

For the past week, I haven't felt well. I'm filled with confusion and the feeling of being alone. Right now I don't really enjoy anyone's company, except a few people. Last Thursday, I couldn't stop crying. I just couldn't. I looked at myself in the mirror. I wondered who it was that was crying … a fat, ugly person crying. I then noticed it was me. I have noticed I put myself down a lot. I don't know why. I just do. I've never thought of suicide or hurting myself, but I have thought about death before. Like, what happens after it? Is judgment passed on us based on our actions? If so, would I end up in hell? Also, I miss my friend a lot. She moved about two or three years ago, but I still miss her. I talk to her through social media. I read her journals and see what is happening. Sometimes I feel like I should be there to comfort her or feel happy because she's happy. I'm really confused right now. I lie to my family about how I act. I lie to my acquaintances too. Through all this lying, have I lost who I really am? Probably not, but it still bothers me.

My head hurts, and so does my heart. Look at me … I'm pathetic … seeking guidance on something. I am usually fine alone. And I cry! What's wrong with me? I also have a secret no one knows. I don't want to tell anyone about it or even mention it! Then there is also the fact that I try my best in school. But sadly, it's never good enough. I never talked to Mom about this either. I'd much rather keep all of this a secret … no one *needs* to worry about me. I'm fine … hopefully. But I can't stop thinking about why I feel this bad. I have a test today. I wonder if my teacher will understand. What will others say? Oh, he skipped classes? Is that what they will think? I don't want my parents to know this or anyone else.

Me

Tell Me Your Story

Senior Girl
Feeling Reflective

Reading this letter from one of my former students put a smile on my face. I actually started chuckling aloud when I thought about this very dry, humorous young girl who always made me laugh. She was never a discipline problem. She was her own problem. She was lots of fun. She could not separate fun from learning and therefore created her own scenario.

She spent several hours in my office talking. Each time she failed another course, she felt lousy—yet she never did anything about it. She was slowly losing the opportunity to graduate with her senior class. She continued to make the wrong choices. She did not understand the consequences. Doomsday came. I had to tell her that she was not eligible for graduation. For the last time, we reviewed her credits. Seeing her grades in black and white made reality set in. She cried for a few moments. We talked about her options. The next day, she made the decision to complete her education at the adult school, and she did it! She offered to write this letter, and I was thrilled to print it. Thanks, __, I am really proud of you!

I am a nineteen-year-old student attending adult school. Let me tell you how it all began and how I ended up here …

I thought high school would be four years of fun, but was I wrong. Freshman year started off good. Sophomore year was when I decided I could get my work done and still have all the fun I wanted. I would get home from school and go hang out with friends. I would do some homework but leave the rest. That was not the best thing to do 'cause when I got my report card, all I saw were Ds and Fs.

Not doing what I was supposed to do my sophomore year really messed up my junior year. I had to take classes over and try to do well in my junior classes. I always told my mom and everyone else that things would change, but they never did. Things just got worse. When I got my report cards, they were mostly Fs. By the end of my junior year, I got the worst possible news anyone could get. I was told I could not graduate with my class.

All I wanted to do was be a teenager and have fun. Worrying about having fun instead of doing well in school was the worst thing I could do. It was not that I couldn't do it because I—and everyone else—knew I could, but I just wanted to have fun. Because of the choice I made to have fun, I was not able to graduate with my class.

I was upset, but I finally realized that fun time was over. I became an adult, and I am now doing what I should have done a long time ago. Going to school is the best thing to do. You need to have a high school diploma to get a good job. You can't always have fun. Getting your high school diploma is the best thing to do. So save the fun for later.

Tell Me Your Story

Senior Girl
Feeling Perplexed

How long can a family survive addiction?

Dear Me,

When I was in grammar school, my parents decided to separate from each other. I was nine years old when the transition began. Even though divorce in America is very common, it takes a different toll on each family. In my situation, I was extremely lucky growing up. My parents both worked full-time and made a good life for my younger brother and me. I lived in a two-story home that my mother decorated beautifully.

You never actually realize how fortunate you are until it's not quite the same anymore. Growing up, I was a daddy's girl. My dad and I had a special bond that I thought could never be broken. My dad was an extremely smart man—with an open mind and much to share with the world. He had an aura about him. When he walked in the room, he made people smile. To me, that's something that cannot be learned. My father taught me so many important lessons in life, even if he didn't notice that he was.

My parents became separated because my dad was an alcoholic and refused to admit it. My mother tried as hard as she could to keep things together, but it was impossible in the end. Throughout the years, my father has been in rehabilitation centers and hospitals, and now his problems stretch so much farther than his addiction. This wasn't so much a crisis as it was a struggle.

Watching my father change over the years tainted me as a person. Going from spending every day with him and learning new things to not seeing him and watching him change into this man I don't know was frustrating and confusing. This separation led to a move from a large house into a smaller house that I did not like, new schools and friends, and a whole new lifestyle that I wasn't ready for. Witnessing someone you looked up to and praised become a self-centered individual who no longer feels the need to teach and educate others is perplexing and difficult to adjust to.

When I was younger, I thought I had a flawless life that would never change; obviously that isn't the case. The struggle to adapt to my new life has made me realize so much. It opened my mind to a whole new way of thinking and seeing things in more than one way.

Some people are blessed with what seems to be perfection their whole lives, and they never undergo serious heartaches or struggles. Those of us who do shouldn't be considered unlucky or unfortunate; we are privileged to be able to experience different aspects of what we call life and what we make of it. Going through this change has made me realize that life is what we make of it. Wherever I end up, I will always keep in mind that I made it happen for myself—and I have found my way through many obstacles along the way.

Tell Me Your Story

Senior Girl
Feeling Confused

This seventeen-year-old is trying to decide if she should break up or stay in her year-old relationship. Making this decision is difficult for her.

Ps and Cs of _____

Pros

- My first real boyfriend
- His hugs make me feel secure.
- When I kiss him, I still get butterflies.
- He doesn't care what anyone thinks about him.
- I love his family.
- I am so comfortable around him.
- I feel like I can be myself and not have to worry about impressing anyone.
- Sometimes he knows me better than I know myself.
- When he is affectionate, it's the best feeling in the world.
- We can talk about anything.
- When he says, "I love you," I know he means it.
- He may not always act like he loves me, but somehow I just know he does.
- He's my best friend.
- I love him so much.
- He is my weakness.

Cons

- Inexperienced
- Even though he's joking, he can hurt my feelings.
- He's not always affectionate.
- Sometimes it seems like he doesn't care about me.
- He doesn't know what girls really want.
- He has a hard time putting his feelings into words or actions sometimes.
- He acts differently when we are with people and when we are alone.
- I compliment him more than he does me.
- I express my feelings more than he does.
- It's going to be one of the hardest things to do if we break up.
- If we do break up, I want him to realize how much I mean to him.
- I feel like he is taking me for granted.
- He doesn't know when to be serious.

Tell Me Your Story

_____
_____
_____
_____
_____
_____
_____
_____
_____
_____
_____
_____
_____
_____
_____
_____
_____
_____
_____
_____
_____
_____
_____
_____
_____
_____
_____
_____
_____
_____
_____
_____

Feeling Heartbroken

This intelligent, lonely, sad, confused, angry girl faced a multitude of emotions.

It breaks my heart to end a friendship over a guy, which is why I didn't do it. But for her to be acting the way she is with him after she knows how much it hurt me is wrong. Why would she want to be with a guy who she knows will cheat and hurt her? I think I might hate her. Hate is a really strong word that I hardly ever feel for anyone or anything. I was always the person everyone came to unburden themselves of their problems. I was always willing to listen to them … just listen … not judge. Then all I did is worry every night about whether their mother was hitting them or whether their father was drunk. They thought I had the perfect family life. I don't. No one does. But who cares about my problems?

He prefers her because she will put out, and because she is skinny and well-endowed. No matter how hard I try, I can't change the way I look. I'm tired of trying to get us back together. She makes me feel like crap. I'm no longer looking forward to my future. I'm always let down. My parents set impossible standards for me. Just because I always laugh, people think I'm happy, but that's a front against people finding out how unhappy I really am. I'm tired of helping people. I feel like I've used up my magic, and now I can't help myself. I hate being the first child. I'm not taking the calculus exam because I couldn't get myself to focus enough on studying. I can't believe I just opened up to a stranger (LOL). Well, not a stranger but someone I don't know like the back of my hand, which I actually don't know that well—or at all really.

This was the first year where I actually didn't try my hardest on my English essays because I thought the guys I liked were more important. Is it possible to die of a broken heart? I can't believe how stupid I have been my senior year. How could she do that to me? She was supposed to be my best friend? I hate that I was so understanding about it when it hurt so much! Why do I want to teach when from what I've seen no one wants to be taught?

Everyone tells me that I am prettier than her, but why didn't he think so? She's not even his type. They have nothing in common. Deep inside, I hope that she messes up in college. I hate feeling that way. I once considered using cocaine because I heard it helps you lose weight. I can't wait to go away this summer—away from all this. I hate the way I look. Sometimes, especially lately, I wish I never came to this town. I belong on a farm. I don't like her eyebrows. I don't know how that's relevant, but it makes me feel better saying it.

He was the first guy I liked who I could ever see myself with for life. He was so much like me, except for the fact that he didn't understand half my words and constantly stuttered. He wasn't that stupid though; he, just like many others, never applied himself.

I don't want to graduate from high school alone. I feel like I've lost my drive for everything.

T
e
l
l

M
e

y
o
u
r

S
t
o
r
y

Senior Girl
Feeling Thankful

This writing comes from a very special girl's senior memory book. Her father was her role model. Academically, she maintained good grades. Emotionally, she was falling apart. Through her high school years, she made some very poor choices. She could have easily kept going in the wrong direction, but she chose to turn herself around. In the following letter, she thanks her father for always being there for her. To those readers who doubt their parenting skills, this letter may give you some hope.

Dear Dad,

I don't know where to start. There are so many things that I want to say to you, but I don't know how to say them. Well, I guess I want to tell you some things that I've had on my mind for a long time now. First of all, I want to thank you for everything that you have done for me. I want you to know that I truly appreciate everything that you have done for us.

Every day, I realize more and more how much you sacrifice for me, _____, and _____. You stayed with us when Mom left. You did your best to raise us, and I think you did a great job. Thank you for giving me a safe, warm, clean place to live. Thank you for sacrificing your wants and needs so I could have a better life. Thank you for teaching me what you know. Thank you for always making dinner. Thank you for always helping me solve my problems. Thank you for sending me to college and buying me a new computer. Thank you for everything I forgot to mention. Thank you for loving me.

You're not like any other father. You raised us to be independent and think differently from others. You taught us about your experiences—good and bad. Instilled in my memory are many of your "wise" sayings. It might seem like I don't remember them, but I do. I look back on them almost every day. I know there have been many times that I should have listened to you when you told me to do something, but I guess I just had to make the mistake for myself. I'll try to listen to you more. You always said to us, when we realize that you were right about the things you told us about, it would be too late. But I've already realized that you were right about many things, and it's not too late. You're still around for me to tell you that I've realized that I have been wrong about many things. For everything that I have been wrong about, I'm sorry. I know that I have caused you a lot of grief over the years. I'm sorry that I worried you and gave you pain. I'll try my best not to worry you anymore.

Dad, I just want you to know how much you mean to me because I know I don't express it much. You honestly are one of my biggest role models. Everyone is always telling me how wonderful you are and that you are a very wise man. I agree with every one of them. I'm going to do my best to succeed in college, obtain a master's degree, and if possible, a PhD too. I am going to do my best to make you proud. Dad, you are the best father that anyone could ask for. I know that I don't say it much, but I love you.

With all my love,

132

Tell

Me

Your

Story

Senior Boy
Feeling Joyful

After reading this very inspirational college essay, you too will be motivated to live.

There are many things that occurred in my life that really played a role in my present self. All of these things that took place helped mold me into what I am today. The events that took place in my life were unique, yet there was one that changed my life completely. This event was my experience with God on an ordinary night in eighth grade.

My experience was on a September night just like any other. I was playing catch with a couple of people in my neighborhood who I had never noticed before. I was throwing the ball around when my mom drove up with her friend. She told me that she was going to my grandmother's house, but I didn't want to go. At that very moment, a man named Bob came out. He started to talk to her, and when they ended their conversation, she told me to stay at the Bible study he was holding that night.

I stayed at the Bible study and listened to them sing songs about God and talk about the Bible. At first, I felt out of place, but as they ended the study, they started to sing again. Bob told me to close my eyes and listen to the words in the songs. As I did this, a strange feeling surrounded me that I had never experienced before. I wanted to have more of this feeling, and when I told Bob about it, he said that it was God's presence. He also said that this presence was always at their Bible studies. From that moment on, I went to every Bible study that I could, and I felt the presence more and more. As I felt the presence more, I felt myself grow closer to God. I changed myself in many ways. Many things that I changed were things that I shouldn't have been doing anyway.

This experience changed me in so many ways. I became more joyful. I stopped cursing almost completely. My faith in God has helped me through so many things in my life, including my parents' and siblings' deaths. If I didn't have faith in God, I think that I would have lost my mind. I think that I would have even tried to kill myself. I believe that people kill themselves and that they take drugs because they feel alone and feel that they have no other escape from the pain. I feel that way because of my strong faith in God. I have grown so close to Him. He's like a friend who is always there for me and won't let me go through anything without help.

As one can clearly see, I didn't go through my life alone. I had someone by my side throughout the good and bad times, guiding me on a path that leads to eternal joy. Everyone can have a friend like this. The only thing that has to be done to get a friend like this is prayer. Not many people realize how easy it is to solve problems and disputes, which I believe are the causes of all the wars in the world today. The feeling of God is the one experience that no one could ever forget, and this experience has touched and changed my life in so many ways. It's my motivation for living.

T
e
l
l

M
e

Y
o
u
r

S
t
o
r
y

Senior Boy
Feeling Scared

This is an article written by one of my seventeen-year-old students in the local newspaper. This brave young man returned to school six weeks after surgery for testicular cancer. He chose to remain in his senior health class even though the topic of discussion was testicular cancer and breast cancer. Within two days, he became so angry with the reaction of his peers that he decided to write an anonymous letter to his classmates. He sat in my office and verbally relived the details of his nightmare.

The next day, he came in with a three-page letter. The health teacher had agreed to read the letter to the class. He sat in the back of the room. I sat in the front of the room. Listening to his letter were thirty seniors (males and females). As the teacher read this emotional letter, you could hear a pin drop. Tears began to flow. When the teacher finished reading, there was silence until a voice from the back of the room said softly, "It's me. I have cancer." He cried as his classmates consoled him. It was a very healing moment.

During a recent health class, I sat in total disbelief at the immaturity level displayed by my peers toward testicular cancer and breast cancer. There were so many comments from kids who probably knew nothing about how cancer affects someone emotionally and physically. I used to be like them—laughing and commenting on things I knew nothing about. But now I know a lot about cancer because I was diagnosed with testicular cancer three months ago.

When I first realized something was wrong, I thought it was nothing and it would go away. I soon realized it wasn't going to go away, and I had to do something. I had to tell somebody. But how do you tell somebody that you have a lump—a mass of some sort—on your left testicle? It's embarrassing.

It took me two weeks to figure out how to tell someone, but I finally did. I told someone who I loved and who I knew loved me unconditionally: my mom. I knew she would be there to help me get through this. Then I went to the doctor. After I was checked, the doctor told me it might be cancer. I broke down crying. The doctor also said I would have to go for surgery to remove the tumor and to see if it was cancer. If it was, they were going to have to remove my testicle along with the tumor. But that possibility didn't sink in because I was trying to convince myself that it wasn't cancer.

When I woke up after the surgery, my worst nightmare became reality. I was told the tumor was malignant and that my left testicle had been removed. At first, I didn't accept the fact that I had cancer. I went into denial and acted like nothing was wrong. The only thing I was worried about was what people would think. *What will girls think when they find out that I only have one testicle? What will they say? How will they act? Will they still want to be with me?* I must have asked myself those questions at least a million times in my head. I finally realized that if that matters to a girl, if she won't be with me because of that, then she's not the girl for me.

Then one day, it hit me. I realized I had cancer and became really depressed. I broke down crying. For the next two weeks, my depression worsened. I couldn't eat or sleep. It was like I wasn't alive. I was existing, but I was not functioning. That's a scary place to be. Eventually I snapped out

T
e
l
l

M
e

Y
o
u
r

S
t
o
r
y

of it. I guess it was due to my friends and especially my mom. They were always there for me and helped me focus on other things. At my next appointment, the doctors said there were no signs of cancer in my body. What a relief!

I just want to get on with my life, but I can't because every month for several years, I have to go for a checkup to see if the cancer has returned. If it does come back, I know I will be more scared than ever because I'll have to undergo chemotherapy—and that scares the heck out of me because I know what chemo does to your body. I don't want that to happen to me. I just want all of this to be over. Before cancer, I really wouldn't open up to people. I had friends and talked to a lot of people, but I didn't let anyone see the real me. Now I've changed.

Tell Me your Story

_____
_____
_____
_____
_____
_____
_____
_____
_____
_____
_____
_____
_____
_____
_____
_____
_____
_____
_____
_____
_____
_____
_____
_____
_____
_____
_____
_____
_____
_____

Senior Boy
Feeling Passionate

Love always wins! Dreams can come true!

Growing up, I would say that I had a very rough childhood. I was born addicted to heroin, and many who had contact with me in those early years thought that my life would be difficult and that it would be hard for me to overcome the effects of the addiction. Indeed, they were correct. But I was fortunate. After eighteen months, a loving couple became my foster parents. They later adopted me and became my mother and father. They helped me get through the hard times and made life easier for me. They gave me a home, a good education, and love. But most of all, they gave me a loving family. My mother and father always supported me. In elementary school, I was placed in special education classes, which continued throughout high school. As of today, I found great success in in-class support classes.

When I was five, I found my passion and drive in musical theater. When I was on stage, I wasn't myself. I wasn't the boy with a learning disability or the little adopted child with no confidence. When the lights went up, I was an actor—a star—and all eyes were on me. I loved it. I had finally found where I belonged.

I felt secure until my world came crashing down. The news that my mother had ovarian cancer was hard for me—and so was life once again. I was ten years old, and all I could think was, *Mommy is going to die. Mommy is going to die.*

Instead of curling up and crying all the time, I found that trying to be the cool kid in school was my outlet. I wanted to be the kid who all the other kids wanted to be. Though I never cried in public, deep inside, I was insecure and scared. I was scared to face reality. But by the time I reached eighth grade, my attitude changed again. My mother was growing weaker, and I decided that I couldn't pretend anymore. I had to be true to myself.

Although my mother was getting sicker and sicker, my life was slowly getting together. My mother died of ovarian cancer just one day before my sixteenth birthday. Even though her death was painful, I found that I have a new motive in life. After her death, I finally realized that she instilled in me what she would consider the four keys to having a successful life. Those keys are opportunity, self-confidence, courage, and wisdom. With those four tools in me, and the help and love of my father, I am proud to say that I've become a self-motivated young man once again—and a young man who knows what he wants to accomplish in life.

Theater is my passion. I live for the spotlight. People have told me that I was always smiling and dancing before I could remember. However, my interest didn't peak until my middle school drama teacher insisted that I try out for the spring musical. After thinking about it, I remembered the fun I had doing various shows.

On the day of the tryout, I ended up auditioning. I got a very good role. Ever since then, I've been doing shows. Each time I am on the stage, it's for my mother. She's my motivation. In the future, my goal is to one day be on Broadway and possibly end up in Los Angeles doing movies. I honestly believe that if I use the four keys to success, my dream will come true. Theater is my goal, my dream, and my focus. I live for the stage, the lights, and the audience. I love it all!

Tell Me Your Story

Senior Girl
Feeling Grateful

The following is a college essay written by a young girl whose mother was diagnosed with cancer. She was just eleven when her mother learned of her diagnosis.

The greatest gift of all is love. Love is what my mother gave to me. My mother was born on _____. She was the greatest person I have ever known, and I am proud to be her daughter. My mom was an extremely caring, loving, and positive human being. Before my twin brother and I were born, mom worked for _____. Her job was very, very daring. She was a telephone linesman who climbed the telephone poles without hesitation. She proved that she was truly a courageous woman. In later years, she chose to be a little less daring and worked in the office as a customer service representative.

She was blessed with a beautiful set of twins: one girl and one boy. My mom was always very supportive of my brother and me. She was a hands-on mom. When I was younger, my mom would bring me for dance lessons on Saturday mornings. My dance lessons continued for five years. Mom was with me every step of the way!

When my brother played baseball, my mom was at every game. When I became involved in chorus, she sat through every one of my shows. As an active member of the PTO, my mom knew how important it was for us to have memories of those years, so she had the school buy the chorus individual shirts for graduation.

Getting the best education was most essential to mom. She would help us with our homework every night. She made sure that we understood everything. My mom was all my brother and I knew. My father moved out when we were five years old, and from then on, we only saw him on weekends. But that never slowed my mom down. We traveled all over New York, often eating hot dogs and having fun watching the Mets or Yankees play.

My mom was the highlight of my life. She was my best friend. I could tell her anything. She fixed all my problems and made my life a lot of fun. My fun slowed down on _____. It was one of the saddest days of my life. My mom was diagnosed with lung cancer. She was admitted to the hospital. I began to stay with my grandma. It was a change because I went from living across the street from school to having to wake up two hours earlier to take two buses to get there.

Every day my mom was in the hospital, I was in touch with her in some way. We were in touch every day: writing letters, talking on the phone, or visiting in the hospital. My mom was released from the hospital and we all stayed with my grandma. Every ten days, she was sick because she was getting chemotherapy, but that didn't stop her from having fun and spending time with my brother and me.

Mom was readmitted to the hospital. Her lung cancer had spread to the brain. I became very sad. My problems seemed to be going from bad to worse. On _____, my mom passed away. That was the worst day of my life. I couldn't do anything but cry. My mom had the biggest impact on my life. She was all I was used to, my everything, and now she was gone. I became very depressed.

142

Tell Me Your Story

I finished sixth grade in New York, and then I moved to New Jersey with my dad. That was a real change for me. I wasn't used to living with him for a while, and that was something to get used to. But my mom taught me how to be patient, loving, and caring. She gave me a very strong faith. She taught me that if things were ever too rough, I always had God to lean on.

It is hard to think about prom and graduation coming up and her not being with me. I could never have imagined life without her. I still don't want to, but I have to. I am now a seventeen-year-old senior, and even though my greatest inspiration is not here to see me dressed up for the prom or walking down the aisle in my cap and gown at graduation, she is always in my heart and is watching over me now and forever. She taught me how to love … the greatest gift of all … and for that, I am forever grateful!

Tell Me Your Story

Senior Boy
Feeling Emotional

Growing up with ADHD and dyslexia was—and continues to be—a struggle.

Growing up for me was fun, strict, and abnormal … a typical Italian family. I was raised in a pretty strict way. As a kid, I couldn't sit still or concentrate. I was hyperactive, and my parents knew something was different. If I did something wrong, my parents would discipline me by hitting me. It wasn't abuse; it was just tradition. The hitting never worked for me. I would just do the same things over again. It was like I didn't care or feel the pain.

Later on, I was diagnosed with ADHD and dyslexia. To this day, I have trouble in class. I can't write or read script. I can't concentrate or sit still for periods of time. Of course, the thing that gets me in trouble most is that I can't shut up. I say things without thinking. I've gotten into trouble because of that—a lot of trouble. I'm not someone who can sit there and hold in my words and anger. I usually have to hit something: doors, walls, desks, windows, cars, anything within reach. I think that's why I'm so good with my hands. I always have to fix things I break.

Everything got me mad. I was too emotional for a long time. What people said affected the way I lived. For example, when I got made fun of for taking medicine for my ADHD, I stopped taking it. I refused to take anything, even if it helped me. I couldn't stand not being liked. Things other people could blow off, like they were nothing, I took to heart. It's a strength and a weakness at the same time. I could talk to people and put smiles on their faces, even when they were faced with death. It was truly a gift from God. Yet I hurt. I would cry over people who were less fortunate than me. I couldn't stand people being sad. Sometimes I made it worse, not on purpose, but out of ignorance. I have a lot of compassion for people. It was always there. I pretty much grew up in a hospital. My mother is a registered nurse and does chemotherapy. I always met her patients and tried to talk to them. I tried to talk to anyone.

Using all my energy in sports, especially soccer and gymnastics, was my way out of this world. I couldn't do baseball. There wasn't enough movement. While I was standing there, waiting for the ball, I used to play in the sand or bite on my glove, which tasted good at the time. One time when they put me at second base, I was playing in the sand. The ball was hit. I got up, got the ball, tagged second, and threw to first. My parents realized that I needed something else! Soccer is what I was best at. I was very fast and had great footwork. My father taught me everything I know. I credit everything to him and to my family. I wouldn't be anywhere without them.

High school was horrible: two-hour classes, the cliques, and sports politics. I get angry very easily. My teachers made me mad. Well, only a few, but everyone gets those kinds of teachers who abuse their authority over you. The only problem is I couldn't take it. Trips to guidance were regular for me. It was the only place I could speak freely and act freely … to get my anger out.

Mrs. D. helped me with a lot of things—not just inside school but outside too. When my sister left for college, it was devastating. She and I were closer than anything. Her being twelve hours away

Tell Me your Story

at college made me feel alone. The only thing that helped me was Christ. Being a Christian in a public high school isn't exactly easy. You get ridiculed for praying or saying anything about Christ. I got sick of it and didn't want anything to do with Christ. It was the worst mistake I could have made. Without Christ, I was truly alone. It hurt. Friends dragged me deeper into drinking, and I just drank at parties to forget everything. It never worked. (I just woke up puking my lungs out with no one there to comfort me.) I had five true brothers in Christ who really helped me. They helped me get back on my feet and got me going again. Without them, I probably wouldn't be as good as I am today.

Things went great after I reaccepted Christ into my life. The need for dressing for other people, drinking, being cool, and caring about what other people thought of me disappeared. I asked God to help me with control of my life, including my disability, my anger, and my thoughts. He helped me understand a lot more and gave me knowledge to help people.

Around that point, Mrs. D. started to bring me in to talk with other students. I'm not trying to boast or anything, but I helped a lot of kids with different problems—at home and at school. They just needed to talk. Getting through high school was a huge struggle for me. Well, I should say it is still a struggle since I am in my senior year. Sometimes you just have to sit back, look at your life, and see what is missing. What is it for you? For me, it was Christ.

Tell Me Your Story

Senior Girl
Feeling Wise

It's never too late!

Dear Me,

I am eighteen. Since I was fourteen, I've been in _____High School. During my first three years of high school, I had my share of friends, enemies, and boyfriends. Since my freshman year, I took school for granted. I didn't take it seriously. Every year, I said, "I have another year. I will do better."

I'm a senior, and I realized that I messed up. During the summer before senior year, I grew up and matured. Some people might not have realized it because I don't really open up all the way, but I know I did. I had my best cousin tell me I matured, and my best friends agreed. It meant the most to me when the one person who actually tried to help me during high school said that I matured. That person was my guidance counselor. She helped my brother make it through high school, and she's helped me. That's how I know I've matured.

I used to be one of those students who slept during class and never listened to announcements. I just didn't really care. School wasn't a big thing for me. Now that I am a senior, I realize how much I messed up. I could have done so much better. I know I could have if I had just set my mind to do so. I was trying to have fun and mess with boys; school was the last thing on my mind.

School is now the first thing on my mind. I was always so caught up in what people thought of me and how I could make everyone happy. I didn't really focus on myself and my happiness. That's what is supposed to be the main thing you do. You worry about yourself and do the best you can to make yourself happy way before you think of pleasing anyone else.

When I had boyfriends, I would always try to change myself—or I would do things to make them happy, which wasn't quite so exciting for me. I did those things because I wanted them to be with me and be happy with me. I learned that if you're not happy in a relationship, you can't just stay with the person just because he wants to be in it. You have to have the love and willingness to care for that person. If you don't have that, then you don't have a relationship. Learn what you like and look for that in the guy or girl. You have to know yourself inside and out in order to give yourself to that person fully. If you don't know yourself, then you can't help someone get to know you.

School is a big deal as a teen. You have big things going on and so much to deal with. School, sports, and boyfriends/girlfriends are one thing, but you also have family and friend issues. What should you do with all the stress? Don't just suck it up and deal with it. Writing down your feelings is a way to tell someone your problems without having to group all your words together. It's also a good way to help solve your problems.

Read over everything you write and think about it—one problem at a time. No one can give you better advice than yourself. During high school, you prepare yourself as a person for the real world to come after high school. It's no joke when they say, "Life is short. Don't take it for granted." It is a true statement. My high school years flew by. I still can't believe I'm graduating soon. Prom is

Tell Me Your Story

coming up. I thought I had more time to plan stuff out. Time is limited. It gets so stressful. That's why you have to make sure you do everything the way it is supposed to be done. Set your hopes, dreams, and future high, so that when it finally hits you that it's almost too late, you have to work twice as hard. But hopefully it won't be too late.

You think that high school is supposed to be fun and parties? Yeah, have your fun, but always remember what's more important. Is it worth messing up your life at such an early age to fit in or be cool? No, I don't think so. Drinking and doing drugs are fun at the time, but in reality, they really catch up to you in the long run. Do you have to be drunk or on drugs to have fun and be around your friends? No, because you're not always going to be drunk or under the influence of drugs. Why must you spend your money on stuff that isn't even worth it? Spending money day after day to feel that "good feeling" adds up. When you need money, you have none.

Friends will show they care and say they'll always be there, but there's always one person who screws up in the end. Then what? Do you think all your friends are going to do it? As a senior, it has happened to me. It can happen at any time. Don't stress it. I haven't and I won't because I know who my true friends are. I know who will be there till the end. I realized friends really do come and go—even the ones you call "ride or die." Always stick to your hand—meaning all five fingers—to count your *friends*. There is nobody else out there to help you find out who's real and who's fake. It's up to you to decide who is real and fake. Remember life is a gamble—just know how to play it!

Tell Me your Story

153

Senior Girl
Feeling Hopeful

This resilient seventeen-year-old has proven that she is a survivor. She wrote this essay for a scholarship awarded by DYFS (Division of Youth and Family Services).

My name is _____. I am seventeen years old, and I have been residing in foster care under the guardianship of my grandmother for more than four years. I was born in _____ where I lived with my grandmother, great-grandmother, and occasionally, my mother.

In the beginning, I wasn't around my mother much because she was only sixteen when she gave birth to me, and she felt that there were better things to do than to take care of me. Then when she was introduced to a man who she thought she was in love with, all of a sudden, I was her daughter—and I was to live with her. She decided to move out of _____ into _____ with my future stepfather. My great-grandmother fought and argued for her to leave me with her, but she insisted on taking me with her. That decision was the worst one she could have made for me.

When I was four, my stepfather began touching me inappropriately. At that age, I had no idea that it was wrong, but I always had a bad feeling when he did it. As I got older, the contact got worse and more violent. He began beating me obsessively when I did something wrong or even if he was just angry. Every week I would show up at school with a new bruise, a black eye, or cuts and scratches.

When I was about six or seven, he began having intercourse with me. He would sometimes bribe me to do it or beat me if I didn't. I tried to tell my mother, but she was always too busy being drunk to see it or believe it. For years, I tried to figure out what I could do to get away from him, but it never happened.

In 199_, the three of us and my younger brother were in a car accident. We each had a lawsuit against the driver and won. I was awarded several thousand dollars in the end, and it was supposed to be put away for college. For the first few years, it was. When my mother couldn't feed her addiction anymore and my stepfather's issues couldn't keep him a job, she cashed in and spent every last penny. Since then, I have not had any money to put toward college.

In the summer of _____, there was a fight at our home. The police were called and questioned me that night. I'll never forget that defining moment when they asked, "What is your relationship with your stepfather like?"

When I attempted to answer, he walked by the door. Struck with fear, I choked and wasn't able to say anything. That's when they knew something was wrong. They took me down to police headquarters and began questioning me. It took until four o'clock the next morning for them to finally drill it out of me. They immediately went to the house, arrested him, and sent me to his parents' house to live. It turned out that they didn't want me, and they sent me to live with his sister. Of course, she found a reason to get rid of me also.

My grandmother stepped in and told DYFS that she would take me in. She fought relentlessly in both _____ and ____ until she was able to receive full custody of me in the summer of

Tell Me Your Story

_____. Since then, I have lived with her. In the summer of _____, I gave birth to my now two-year-old son. After finding out that I was pregnant, my grandmother placed me in a maternity home, and she retook custody of me the day I left the hospital. We have had many ups and downs, good times and bad, fights and friendly conversations, and we are still struggling.

Shortly after my son was born, my grandmother and I moved to _____ to live with my great-grandmother because she was no longer able to care for herself. To further help our growing family, my grandmother's fiancé moved in with us also. In October of last year, my unfit mother gave life to a premature baby girl who my grandmother also took in.

Living in foster care for so many years has taught me a lot of things. It has taught me how to be mature and responsible and how to prove those qualities to myself. It has also shown me how to not take life for granted because at any moment, life can completely turn around. Most importantly, foster care has taught me to never give up. Even when things are horribly bad, there will be a brighter day on the way.

I have applied for this scholarship so that I will have a chance to pursue my dream of moving on to college and not give up on what life has to offer. I refuse to believe that my dreams are too far out of reach or too expensive to afford. I will go to college, and I will graduate with a nursing degree. Being in foster care has given me a strong, determined attitude.

Tell Me Your Story

Graduates
Reflect on Yesterday

Tell Me Your Story

Graduate Boy

The following is a poem written by a special young man about a year after graduation. His words were written to a friend who was grieving the loss of her parents. There is no one who understood what she was going through better than he did. These two exceptional adolescents were both orphaned at the age of fifteen. They played instrumental roles in our bereavement group. They are an inspiration for all!

Hard to Go On
To my friend

You and I have both experienced the same.
We both know that life isn't just a game.
We've been through a lot of hard times,
Very often just begging for a sign,
But we realized we have to do it on our own,
For reasons that are not yet known,
Why did this have to happen to us?
Is this one of life's little musts?
But we have to go on.
We have to be strong.
If we don't, then we are like all the rest.
We can't keep living our lives so depressed.
We have been chosen for something great,
We've been given the power to make our own fate.
Although many are gone, we are alive.
And we can still order our croutons on the side.
So just keep your head up—and don't ever give up.

Tell Me Your Story

Graduate Girl

She was only eighteen at the time—one month after graduation. She was searching desperately to feel wanted. She had been in outside counseling for a few months. She put herself in a very compromising situation. She thought she was pregnant. She wasn't.

The following is a poem she wrote depicting what her life would have been like had she been pregnant. If you are in this same spot in life, please know that you are not alone. Get the help you need. Talk to a responsible adult. Do it now! Please make good choices for you.

Sitting on a Porch

Sitting on a porch watching the world around me
while a baby cries next to me, held by a complete stranger.
We are so close yet so far.
Do I really know who you are sitting next to me, holding our child?
Across from me are three small children, laughing, tagging, playing.
Beautiful mixed children, half-Asian, half-Hispanic,
not a care in the world, not knowing the thoughts and problems
of their mother and father—more so their mother,
who sees confusion in her life every day.
She was on her way to a career and independence.
But she chose a different path: no marriage, no education, no life,
only twenty-two with four kids and a man.
A man not bound to her by marriage, a man only bound by kids.
Not even a man—still just a boy.
She loves him though—more than he'll ever know.
But does he love her just the same?
Sure he stays at home with the kids while she puts in sixty-hour weeks at a job in retail,
but does he truly appreciate her?
Does he appreciate her soft touch, her caring honesty,
her gracious humility, her charming and mannered ways?
Does he appreciate her even more now that she's carried four of his babies
and does all she can to raise them to be educated and well?
Or does he just not care?
The only valuable thing she had was herself, and unknowingly
she gave it to him; her life was sucked dry.
Where there once was charisma, spunk, and a bubbly personality,
only a speck of her soul is left—no real dignity.
All that beautiful life was taken away, taken away by this man,
this selfish being—no … correction … this boy.
He was her first everything, and in her heart, she wanted him to be
her last everything—to be together forever.
But nothing lasts forever, and life is never fair.
So here I am, sitting on a porch and watching the world around me,
held by that boy I desperately love, watching my life pass me by.

Tell Me Your Story

Graduate Boy

There was a knock on my door. A frantic nineteen-year-old girl whose brother had threatened to commit suicide the night before cried, "Please help!" I looked at the clock. The school day was about to end. The bell would ring in ten minutes. I ran to the physical education class to find her brother. There he was ... just sitting there and waiting to go home. Here is his story.

Dear Me,

Well, it seems as if I've made it to hell and back. I am one of the lucky few to have been through what I've been through and am still able to talk about it. Well, let me say this: I am an addict. There are no limits to this, no ends, no specifics other than what I have already done. For me, to be able to say this is a huge thing. Addiction is a disease of the mind, body, and spirit. It is cunning, baffling, insidious, incurable, and fatal. Although it can be arrested, and recovery made possible, there is not just one road that this disease can take. My story, however, has to do with the use of drugs.

Now, after having to take a good and long look at myself, I know I was an addict long before I picked up a drug. It shows in my attitudes, thoughts, and behaviors. My first drug was nicotine, which I picked up very early. As it turns out, right after I started smoking, which was before I got out of fifth grade, I started drinking and smoking marijuana as a result of the group of people I associated with. I thought it was fun and what everyone did. Little did I know how it would progress.

It started off once in a while, mostly once a month when I had extra money. In the next few years, I got a job. It went from once a month to twice a month, then to twice a week, and then three times a week. By the time it got to three times a week, I was in eighth grade. By that summer, I would put $400 into a party every Monday. Basically, I would work hard to play hard. It turned into the beginning of the end. I ended up spending everything I earned on a fix, and my choices broadened. By my freshman year, I didn't care. I started using any pill I could get my hands on. I would smoke up and drink as much as I could. I stopped doing work, and I was too lazy to even change for gym.

This managed to continue to the end of tenth grade. Then it got drastically worse. I had no more job and very little money. I started to push for people I knew, and I started to use more and more. For the most part, I used everything that came my way, and this turned into me using an ounce of marijuana a day and whatever else I could get my hands on. I used before school, during, and I left early to go and use—not caring what happened to me in that time. I also had a suicide attempt because my girlfriend at the time broke up with me.

For me, though, the end came during the summer of _____. I was still doing what I was doing, but I started doing cocaine too. I was a slave to my habit, but one night, right down the street from my house, I had just gotten done using, and the police showed up on a complaint from my neighbors. I always say that this was the day my life was spared. I was arrested and held with four drug charges. My two sisters came to pick me up from police headquarters, yet even after that, I still used. I kept

T
e
l
l

M
e

y
o
u
r

S
t
o
r
y

going until I had to tell my mother what happened. When I did, I enrolled in counseling and started to attend a twelve-step fellowship.

My court date was scheduled for November, and I had ninety days clean by then, so I was shown leniency. I was on probation under PTI, and my record was to be cleaned after I served one year. Three of the four charges were dropped, and I was to fulfill my counseling. Today, I can look back on all of this and know that I am blessed to have been given the opportunity to know the person I was is no longer here. I put down the drugs and was able to graduate from high school on the honor roll.

I now have close to two years clean. I am no longer a thief, a junkie, useless, or any of the demeaning things this disease can make us. I also know that my family has stuck by me through thick and thin and hasn't left my side at all. I have become a productive member of society. The greatest part about it is that I've walked through hell and back and can still talk about it.

Tell Me Your Story

_____
_____
_____
_____
_____
_____
_____
_____
_____
_____
_____
_____
_____
_____
_____
_____
_____
_____
_____
_____
_____
_____
_____
_____
_____
_____
_____
_____
_____
_____
_____
_____

Graduate Girl

On a cool, brisk October day, a beautiful girl who had graduated the previous June walked through my door with the following writing in her hand. She was a girl I had sat with several times. She promised me that she would write about her experiences in high school, and she did. I am extremely thankful to her for sharing her thoughts with you. Enjoy!

The Ride of Your Life

High school … if you would have asked me about it during my senior year, I would have said something like, "It was the biggest waste of time." And now, after receiving my high school diploma and stepping out into the real world of college and work, I can say it was one of the biggest mountains I had to climb. It was filled with ups and downs and narrow edges to walk across. Yet this mountain, though steep and hard to climb, shaped who I was as a person. After all my experiences in high school, I am one step closer to finding out who I really am.

Freshman year—what a year! Walking into high school that first day was like jumping into a pool and not knowing how to swim. Meeting new people, harder classes, new beginnings, and necessary losses—freshman year was an emotional roller coaster filled with surprises every step of the way.

Sophomore year was even greater than freshman year, and I would probably mark it as the high point of high school. As a sophomore, you finally had a sizable grip on what high school was all about. You pretty much knew everyone and already had a whole bunch of new friendships. You start to have even more fun than you did freshman year. You can hang with all the seniors and go out at night because you weren't a "baby" anymore. My sophomore year was just that, and I would never take any of those memories away.

As I got to junior year, things took a quick turn. All the fun I had sophomore year drastically stopped. I began worrying about college, my future, and my life. My classes got more difficult, and I had no time for anything.

Junior year was the beginning of my first breakdown. I had so much on my plate. I had school, a job, homework, college, and driving to worry about. (That was a big stress for my parents as well!) I had to manage a life and a boyfriend. It felt like it was too much to handle. I started feeling that growing up wasn't what it was cracked up to be. As the year was drawing to a close, the breakdown continued. I tried so hard to do well on my SATs and keep my grade point average and rank up. Competition with peers started getting even heavier. I felt as though I was worthless to everyone. I started realizing that I couldn't wait to get out of high school and start a new life in college.

As I finally stepped into my senior year, I wasn't prepared to face some of the challenges that came my way. Senior year was said to be the best year of your life—with few worries and much partying—but it was a myth. Like seniors, I was stressed in the beginning of the year, applying to colleges and keeping up with my schoolwork. When all my applications were done, I was happy that they were out of the way, but I felt like those two or three months of waiting lasted a lifetime. And when we

T
e
l
l

M
e

Y
o
u
r

S
t
o
r
y

finally started getting letters back from the universities we applied to, devastation came my way. I had been rejected from the school of my dreams. The feeling that I felt when I opened that rejection letter is one that I hope I will never have to feel again: incompetence! After my rejection, senior year just got worse. For four years, I had been involved in many extracurricular activities: honor societies, concert choir, and the high school play. By the end of my senior year, I had managed to quit many of the things I once loved because I felt that it "wasn't worth it." Also, during my senior year, I had gone through an extremely difficult heartbreak that will be with me for the rest of my life. I started to sink deeper and deeper into depression because of the "lack of ability" I thought I had and all the self-confidence issues I endured for most of my life.

When I look back, I realize that high school was just a stepping-stone in my life—a cluster of memories and experiences that will live with me and shape me. Without high school, I wouldn't have been prepared to face the future or the real world. I finally realized that high school was a necessary passage of time, and after my high school experiences, I can say, "Yes, life isn't always gravy, but you learn from it—and you learn to survive." A wise person once said, "You get used to hanging on if you have to." And it's true. And though this reality might scare many of us, I think I realized that once you get used to it, hanging on doesn't seem so hard anymore. I guess it's true that pain only makes you stronger. I just hope that everyone else out there knows it too.

Tell Me Your Story

_____

_____

_____

_____

_____

_____

_____

_____

_____

_____

_____

_____

_____

_____

_____

_____

_____

_____

_____

_____

_____

_____

_____

_____

_____

_____

_____

_____

_____

_____

Graduate Girl

This very exceptional woman was orphaned at fifteen. She is now in her early thirties. She graduated with a bachelor's degree in communications and is writing her life story. Look for her deeply moving autobiography *It's Not Real Until You Write It Down*.

When I was in first grade, my mother sat my sister and me down. My mom and dad told us she had been diagnosed with cancer. I had no idea what it was because I was so young, but my sister understood. I knew it wasn't good news when my sister started crying.

For four years, my mother battled cancer. It started in her breast and spread throughout her body, causing bone cancer. She stayed in a hospital bed in my living room, and my father took care of her while she went through her chemo treatments and radiation.

My mother was a wonderful person. It's hard for me to have a lot of memories since I was so young, but from what I remember and the stories I hear, she was the nicest and most caring person you could ever meet. On _____, my mother passed away at the age of forty-six in our living room. Earlier that day, my father came to my elementary school and picked me up early. He said that Mommy wanted to see me and was having a bad "sick" day. I didn't realize what was happening, but everyone else knew.

Later that night, my whole family was at my house. It was as if she knew what was happening. She waited for everyone to arrive so she could say her good-byes. She told me never to forget her and that she loved me and I would always be her "_____." I fell asleep on my uncle's lap and heard my family telling her to go toward the light.

I fell asleep, and I woke up in my living room. My mother was no longer breathing. My sister was screaming in the kitchen. One uncle was punching the wall, and my other uncle was throwing the garbage cans. My father was outside. Everyone else was scattered everywhere, making phone calls and plans for the wake and funeral. I remember watching her leave my house in a black bag on a stretcher, but I didn't cry. It just wasn't real to me yet. I didn't understand. At her wake, I was outside playing hopscotch. It really was not clear to me yet.

As time went on, I understood what happened. I had my breakdowns, not knowing why this happened to me. About two years later, my sister left for college. When it was just me and my father, I was daddy's little girl to the extreme. Ever since I was little, it was always me and him. My father was so good to me. He trusted me and let me do almost anything I wanted. I always dreamed of dancing with him to "Butterfly Kisses" at my wedding and having him walk me down the aisle and give me away.

When I was in eighth grade, I was scared my dad was going to die because he had had a heart attack earlier in that year. He had to have a quadruple bypass. He came out of the surgery fine! Ever since then, I would open the door to his room every morning to make sure his chest was going up and down. My dad had been a diabetic since he was six and smoked practically his whole life, which made matters worse. My grandmother always said he was just living for my sister and me. When he

Tell Me your Story

realized my sister was going to be okay on her own, he was just living for me until I was older. She says he died of a broken heart.

In _____, I went away to a cheering competition for the weekend. When I got home, my dad said, "Don't kiss me. I'm sick." He sounded horrible and had a really bad cough.

The next morning was a Monday, and I faked being sick 'cause I didn't want to go to school. He said, "Fine. Go back to bed."

All day long, I told him to call the doctor because he was so sick.

He said if he woke up the next day and didn't feel any better, he would go to the doctor. He was *so* stubborn! (That's where I get my stubbornness from.)

The next morning, I woke up and faked being sick again. He asked me to call the doctor. I called his sister and asked her to drive us.

The doctor told him to go straight to the emergency room because he heard water in his lungs. But since my dad was so stubborn, he made us bring him home so he could have lunch first, which he couldn't even eat because he was so sick.

For nine months, my dad was in the hospital. On one occasion, he punched the doctor in the face for taking his blood—and then they made him have his arms tied down. He was in ICU the most, and I remember him having all these tubes and machines hooked up to him. I never wanted to go visit because I couldn't handle seeing him like that.

One time my aunt, uncle, and my sister made me go see him because they said I would be fine. When we got there, I felt really shaky and dizzy. I got myself so worked up, and I had a panic attack. I was sitting in his hospital room and started swaying.

My uncle noticed that my eyes started to fill up with tears and said, "Let's go for a walk."

I got up, took two steps, collapsed, and passed out. When I woke up, I had oxygen up my nose, and I was having my blood pressure checked in a wheelchair.

My sister and aunt told my dad I fell so he didn't worry, but it took something like that for my family to finally believe I couldn't handle going to the hospital. That's why, to this day, I hate hospitals. Unless it's a dying emergency, I won't go.

While my dad was in the hospital, he had severe pneumonia. It took a while, but he was getting better. Since he was heavily sedated and the oxygen to his brain was cut off, his head was messed up. There were times when I visited him with my aunt and uncle, and he didn't even know who we were.

When he saw people climbing the poles in the parking lot, he told us they were racing—and they had been doing it all day. It was really crazy talk. In _____, he was doing really well. They moved him to a rehab center, and we had a family meeting about him coming home and how things would have to change. We were going to need a live-in nurse and make everything wheelchair accessible because he wasn't able to walk. Out of nowhere, he started seeing people coming out of the vents at the rehab facility, and they sent him back to the hospital.

On _____, my father passed away at the age of sixty-nine. I went to school, thinking it was going to be a normal day, and when I got home, I saw my brother's car in the driveway. I knew

T
e
l
l

M
e

Y
o
u
r

S
t
o
r
y

something was up. He never stopped by unexpectedly, especially when no one was even home. I went inside, said hello, and started doing the dishes. I ignored my brother on the couch, trying to avoid the obvious. He told me to come sit down because he needed to tell me something.

When I sat down on the other end of the couch, he said, "We got Dad on the floor we wanted today." He was on the floor where the nurses were supposedly more alert and took better care of the patients.

I said, "Oh, that's good."

"But something happened." My father had to go to the bathroom, and when the nurse came in to help him, he told her to leave him. He would be okay.

When she came back to see if he needed help getting back to the bed, he was on the floor—and not breathing. He had a heart attack, and it took his life.

I looked at my brother and couldn't believe what he had just told me. I asked, "So he's dead?" Almost second-guessing what he had told me.

The phone started ringing, and he answered it.

I knew it was my best friend because we always talked after school.

My brother told her I couldn't come to the phone and that I would call her back, but she heard me crying in the background. I ran into the other room and punched the wall. Not even five minutes later, my best friend was ringing my doorbell. She knew something was wrong. Within fifteen minutes, all my eight girlfriends were with me. That is why we are all so close.

I'll never forget how painful that day was—as bad as the day my mother died—and how each day is just as hard. I am so afraid of losing people I love. Everyone has left me in my house except my dog (with the exception of my sister returning this past summer). That's also why I'm so attached to my dog. She was there for me to cry on, and she never left—unlike my mom and dad (who had no choice) and my sister (who got out as fast as she could).

Life can be unpredictable. One minute, everything is fine—and the next minute everything is in disarray. I had a choice to give up or start over. I took the right path, and I have my parents to thank for that. I know what they would want for me—and it wouldn't be to fail. So each day, I live my life and take one step forward, but I'll never forget my past. My parents are always with me, looking over me, and I just hope one day we'll meet again.

If I feel as though my life isn't real, I start to write it down. When I read the words and feel the emotions begin to stir, it becomes real. This is my life—for real!

Tell Me your Story

Part 2

A Survival Guide for Adolescents, Parents/Guardians, and Teachers

I'm not afraid of storms for I'm learning to sail my ship.
—Louisa May Alcott

Surviving Adolescence

It was a warm, sunny autumn day in New Jersey. The newscaster announced the weather for the day would be ten degrees above normal: 80 degrees, sunny, turning cloudy, and rain later in the day. Beware of strong winds. Take anything in that may get blown away. This turbulent forecast reminded me of a typical day in the life of an adolescent: one minute is sunny, and the next minute is rainy.

In the blink of an eye, a major storm erupts and destroys everything in its path. The following pages respond to the questions that resound over and over again in *Tell Me a Story about This Crazy World Called High School.* They begin with my own definition of adolescence, parenting, and teaching. Next, I created a "bill of rights" to help adolescents and adults understand exactly what they are deserving of. It ends with some practical coping skills to help everyone involved in this fury of confusion survive these tumultuous days.

Adolescence resembles a weather forecast that is always changing: one minute at a time, one hour at a time, and one day at a time. The end result is always unpredictable, but in time, it does end!

Adolescence

Adolescence is a time of growing both physically and mentally … growing into a unique individual whose body and mind have been created through the eyes and ears of one's own self. Adolescence is a time of making life-altering choices … choices that will affect the rest of one's life … choices that will determine the happiness of one's being. Adolescence is a time of discovering one's self … discovering that which makes one truly happy … discovering that one's happiness can only be measured by one's own definition of happiness.

Adolescence is a time of conflict and turmoil within one's self, one's family, and one's friends … conflict and turmoil that may be consumed with oceans of tears … conflict and turmoil that eventually subsides after years of verbal and/or physical confrontations.

Adolescence is a time of parents/guardians slowly letting go … slowly letting go of "control" and allowing the adolescent to gain "control" of himself/herself … slowly letting go in order for the adolescent to develop into an independent young adult. Adolescence is the beginning of discovering the "me" I need to be … because I am … I was … and I will be me yesterday … today … tomorrow … forever!

Remember … when you look into a mirror, only one set of eyes looks back at you forever! Your eyes are the window to your soul! Write a description of who you need to be … as a teenager.

_____

_____

_____

_____

_____

_____

_____

_____

_____

_____

_____

_____

_____

_____

_____

_____

Parenting

The amount of chaos within a family unit depends greatly on the choices an adolescent makes during these trying years. You, as the parent/guardian, are responsible for the safety of your child. Loving, nurturing, and teaching your child is your main concern. Your child, in return, loves you as a parent and respects your wishes … for the most part.

Please remember … your child is in the throes of adolescence where decision-making skills become skewed. The child you thought you raised has gone haywire. Where is that person? He or she is in there … searching for himself or herself … having to make serious choices that will affect him or her for the rest of his or her life. The values and beliefs you taught your child are embedded deep within his or her brain. Your child knows right from wrong.

Your child knows that there are consequences to his or her actions. Your child is in control of his or her own thoughts. Your child needs to learn from his or her own mistakes. Your child needs to grow in order to become an adult. Your child hopes that you will be there if he or she falls—even though he or she doesn't say it! Communication is the key to surviving these times. Listen, talk, and always stick to what you believe in. Remember who you are. Remember what your value system is. Once adolescence is over, the child you once knew will be an adult who will always be your child. Words to live by … I am the parent. I love my child.

Remember—when you look into a mirror, only one set of eyes looks back at you forever! Your eyes are the window to your soul! Write a description of who you need to be … as a parent.

_____

_____

_____

_____

_____

_____

_____

_____

_____

_____

_____

_____

_____

_____

_____

Teaching

Teaching is a responsibility to "teach" vulnerable young people who sit in front of you day in and day out. They look to you for guidance, wisdom, and knowledge. It is more than a job. It is a lifetime commitment to another human being.

Several years ago, when I was studying to be a teacher, I was fortunate to be taught by Dr. Joelna Marcus. I greatly respect her as a human being and as a teacher. It was in her office that I found a profound Chinese proverb: "Give a man a fish, and he'll eat for a day. Teach a man to fish, and he'll eat for a lifetime." It says exactly how I feel. Forty years later, that same quote hangs in my office. It is a part of me forever!

Remember—when you look into a mirror, only one set of eyes look back at you forever! Your eyes are the window to your soul! Write a description of who you need to be as a teacher.

_____

_____

_____

_____

_____

_____

_____

_____

_____

_____

_____

_____

_____

_____

_____

_____

_____

_____

_____

_____

_____

_____

_____

_____

Bill of Rights
Adolescents, Parents/Guardians, and Teachers

Adolescents, empower yourselves. You have the power within you to control each and every situation. Knowing what your rights are will help you survive these difficult years and the rest of your life. The roller-coaster ride of emotions will end. The walls of high school will come down on graduation day, and a new world will begin. Ask anyone who has been your age! Below is your bill of rights. Make these words a part of your everyday vocabulary. Memorize them. They are your bill of rights forever!

I have a right...

to love myself...to be treated with respect...to voice my own opinion...to make my own choices...to be loved...to say "no" without feeling guilty...to express my own feelings...to make my own mistakes...to be listened to seriously...to be happy!

Was there a time when you were assertive and stood up for yourself? How did you feel? How did the other person/persons react? What was the outcome? Was the outcome what you expected?

_____

_____

_____

_____

_____

_____

_____

_____

_____

_____

_____

_____

_____

_____

_____

_____

_____

_____

_____

_____

Parents and guardians, empower yourselves. You have the power within you to control each and every situation. Knowing what your rights are will help you survive these difficult years. The roller-coaster ride of emotions will end. Adolescent years will end, and a new world will begin. You will be the parent of an adult. Ask any parent who has survived these trying years of adolescence! Below is your bill of rights. Make these words a part of your everyday vocabulary. Memorize them. They are your bill of rights forever!

I have a right...

to love myself...to be treated with respect...to voice my own opinion...to make my own choices...to be loved...to say "no" without feeling guilty...to express my own feelings...to make my own mistakes...to be listened to seriously...to be happy!

On the lines below, write about a time that you incorporated your bill of rights into your parenting. Who are you? Where are you? What are you feeling right now?

_____

_____

_____

_____

_____

_____

_____

_____

_____

_____

_____

_____

_____

_____

_____

_____

_____

_____

_____

_____

Teachers, empower yourselves. You have chosen to become teachers. Knowing what your rights are will help you survive this challenging career. You have the power within you to control each and every situation on a daily basis. Your students look to you for guidance and wisdom. You are the positive role models who can change an adolescent's life. Below is your bill of rights. Make these words a part of your everyday vocabulary. Memorize them. They are your bill of rights forever!

I have a right...

to love myself...to be treated with respect...to voice my own opinion...to make my own choices...to be loved...to say "no" without feeling guilty...to express my own feelings...to make my own mistakes...to be listened to seriously...to be happy!

On the lines below, write about a time that you incorporated your bill of rights into your teaching.

_____

_____

_____

_____

_____

_____

_____

_____

_____

_____

_____

_____

_____

_____

_____

_____

_____

_____

_____

_____

Coping Skills
Adolescents, Parents/Guardians, and Teachers

Self-Talk

It's as simple as ABC. *A*ccept yourself for who you are. Love yourself for the unique person you are. *B*elieve in yourself. You have the strength within you to reach any goal. *C*ontrol your thoughts. Positive thinking creates positive energy!

After attending an exceptionally optimistic workshop at the NJEA Convention, I was anxious to share what I learned with my very special third graders. With their approval, we started a new tradition for our morning routine. We would pledge the flag, sing the National Anthem, and recite the affirmation below. Twenty years later, my third graders are now thirty years old. They still remember saying these powerful words.

Try it. Get up each morning and repeat "I can … I can … I can … I like myself … I like myself … I like myself." These simple words repeated each morning just might be what you need to survive this crazy world!

After saying these powerful words on a daily basis, I promise your life will change. New doors will open. You will feel better about yourself. You will like the person you see in the mirror. Use the lines below to write about how your life has changed since you started believing in yourself.

_____
_____
_____
_____
_____
_____
_____
_____
_____
_____
_____
_____
_____
_____
_____

Decision Making

Decision making is simple for some and extremely difficult for others. Look at the steps of decision making below. If you follow the plan, making decisions will become less complex. There are three components to making a sound decision: Identify the problem. Look at your alternatives. Decide your objective. Never lose sight of the goal you want to achieve!

Decision Making

State the problem. (Be honest.)
Evaluate past events. (Be honest.)
Reflect on your future. (Where do you see yourself?)
Explain your goals. (What do you really want?)
Select the best choice. (Be wise!)
Carry out your decision. (Don't second guess yourself.)

What was the last decision you had to make? Were you pleased with the outcome? The next time you have to make a decision, try following the six steps of decision making. What is the problem? What are the alternatives? What is your objective? Write out your plan on the lines below.

_____

_____

_____

_____

_____

_____

_____

_____

_____

_____

_____

_____

_____

_____

_____

_____

_____

_____

Remember that decision making is problem solving. Very often, fear gets in the way of making a decision. Always remember that you are in control of your thoughts. The following scenario captures the impact that allows fear to hinder decision making.

As I was counseling one of my girls who had been harassed throughout her middle school years, she repeatedly spoke of the degrading words that tormented her for three years. After endless hours of outside therapy, she still could not free herself from their reins.

One day, I found a small windup ear that walked. I wound it up. It walked toward her. As she and I laughed at this funny-looking character, I looked at her and said, "Fear is in your ear." I've used that statement several times since then. That windup ear remains in my office to this day.

Have you ever allowed fear to stop you in your tracks?

_____

_____

_____

_____

_____

_____

_____

_____

_____

_____

_____

_____

_____

_____

_____

_____

_____

_____

_____

_____

_____

_____

_____

Conflict Resolution

Conflict resolution resolves conflicts between two people. Both parties involved are on the same playing ground. There is no imbalance of power. Conflict resolution is about figuring out different ways to work through and resolve problems. It is not an easy task. There are a lot of emotions involved. Very often, there are deep-rooted feelings. With time and patience, conflicts can be resolved. There is always an answer. It may not be the answer you want, but there is always an answer.

Resolving a Conflict
Make sure you set ground rules. (This is very important!)
Please listen to each other. (Really listen...don't interrupt each other.)
Look for common interests. (This may be simple...or not.)
Suggest possible solutions to the problem. (Discuss ideas you have thought about.)
Talk about each person's point of views to solve the problem. (Keep an open mind.)
Reach an agreement. (It may or may not be what you hoped for. That is okay!)

Have you ever been involved in a situation where you had to resolve a conflict? Who was involved in the dispute? Were you able to listen to each other's points of view? Were any solutions decided upon? Was there an agreement reached? Try following the six steps to resolving a conflict the next time a conflict arises.

_____
_____
_____
_____
_____
_____
_____
_____
_____
_____
_____
_____
_____
_____
_____
_____
_____

Feelings

Feelings are real. Feelings are rooted deep within you. Feelings fluctuate in degrees from extremely cool to extremely hot. Only you know how you feel. No one has a right to negate your true feelings. If you find yourself losing control, please talk to someone. You can learn how to cope with these feelings. You are not alone.

   Look at the feelings named below and then write about a time when you had that feeling.

Joy_____
_____
_____

Happiness_____
_____
_____

Excitement_____
_____
_____

Anxiety_____
_____
_____

Worry_____
_____
_____

Anger_____
_____
_____

Frustration_____
_____
_____

Shame_____
_____
_____
_____

Where are you on a scale of one to ten with your feelings? What gets you so hot that you are ready to explode? How can you stop yourself before you get to the point of no return? What are your coping skills? What do you do to maintain self-control when faced with a challenge that creates those horrible feelings or sickening arguments?

_____

_____

_____

_____

_____

_____

_____

_____

_____

_____

_____

_____

_____

_____

_____

_____

_____

_____

_____

_____

_____

_____

_____

_____

_____

_____

_____

_____

Life's Toughest Questions

To do good things in the world, first you must know who
you are and what gives meaning to your life.

—Robert Browning

"Life's Toughest Questions" responds to the underlying issues discussed throughout *Tell Me a Story about This Crazy World Called High School*. There are several answers that these very special young people and their parents are in search of. The following pages give an understanding to some of life's most difficult questions.

There is no one solution to all of life's problems. There is no one perfect fit to solve the complexities of life, but there is one simple answer to help begin the healing process: love. No matter how you feel right now, please take the time to read the following pages. Please be open to hearing the words. You deserve to be happy. It can only happen if you allow it to happen. Believe it or not, love always wins!

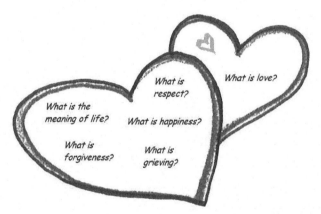

If you look to others for fulfillment, you will never truly be fulfilled.
If your happiness depends on money, you will never be happy with yourself.
Be content with what you have; rejoice in the way things are.
When you realize there is nothing lacking, the whole world belongs to you.
—Lao Tzu

The Meaning of Life

Life is formed by your experiences and supported by your beliefs and values. On the following lines, please write your personal thoughts about the meaning of life as seen through your eyes.

_____

_____

_____

_____

_____

_____

_____

_____

_____

_____

_____

_____

_____

_____

_____

_____

_____

_____

_____

_____

_____

_____

_____

_____

_____

_____

_____

_____

_____

_____

Life

Look at the middle two letters of the word *life*. *If* is a small word that means a lot.

If my life were a TV show, which one would it be? _____

If my life were a movie, which one would it be? _____

If my life were a play, which one would it be? _____

If my life were a book, which one would it be? _____

If my life were a magazine, which one would it be? _____

If my life were a song, which one would it be? _____

If my life were a game, which one would it be? _____

If my life were a color, which one would it be? _____

If my life were a painting, which one would it be? _____

If my life were a mathematical problem, which one would it be? _____

If my life were an historical event, which one would it be? _____

If my life were a food, which one would it be? _____

If my life were a recipe, which one would it be? _____

If my life were a sandwich, which one would it be? _____

If my life were a weather forecast, which one would it be? _____

If my life were a science experiment, which one would it be? _____

If my life were a sport, which one would it be? _____

If my life were a building, which one would it be? _____

If my life were a vehicle, which one would it be? _____

If my life were a piece of furniture, which one would it be? _____

If my life were a piece of clothing, which one would it be? _____

Draw what the meaning of life looks like to you!

Grieving

Grieving is loss. It is the loss of a loved one, a pet, a relationship, a friendship, health, or a job. If you have ever faced the death of a loved one, the death of a friend, a divorce, a serious illness, an accident, or a tragedy, you know what grieving feels like.

Loss is real. Real is painful. It is a painful emotional process that occurs within each of us when we are faced with any devastating loss. It is true heartache. The ache is so deep inside that you can feel your heart bleeding. Sleeping, eating, and concentrating become extremely difficult.

Each person grieves in his or her own way. There is no time line for grieving. After days, months, or years, the pain becomes more tolerable. Acceptance becomes real. Memories are your source of hope. The sun begins to shine again … slowly.

If you are having a difficult time getting through this painful time, please know that there is help. Please talk to someone. On the following lines, write about an experience that you have faced. How did you survive this difficult time in your life?

_____

_____

_____

_____

_____

_____

_____

_____

_____

_____

_____

_____

_____

_____

_____

_____

_____

_____

_____

Remember that you are not alone. Everyone faces extremely difficult times. Please read the powerful words of this very emotional seventeen-year-old whose writing can be found on page 112. It is with gratitude that I share it with you.

Dear Daddy,
I just want you to know that waking up each morning knowing that you're not going to be here has become very difficult for me. But you know what? Every morning I wake up for you because I know I can't give up and I know you won't let me. I just want to be a good person and for you to be proud of me. I'm so jealous of my friends that have fathers because they'll have the chance to walk their daughters down the aisle or kiss them goodnight or just say, "I love you." But every night when I go to sleep I know you're there smiling down on me and I know that you will always be there when I need you. There is so much I want to say to you, to tell you, but all I can think of right now is, "I love you and I miss you so much."

Love always,

Share your thoughts.

_____

_____

_____

_____

_____

_____

_____

_____

_____

_____

_____

_____

_____

_____

_____

_____

_____

_____

_____

_____

_____

Draw what grieving looks like to you!

Respect

Respect is caring about yourself and others. Respect elicits respect. We all have feelings. We all have emotions. We all have hearts. We all bleed red!

Write your definition of respect.

_____

_____

_____   *We all bleed red!*

_____

_____

_____

_____

_____

_____

_____

_____

_____

_____

_____

_____

_____

_____

_____

_____

_____

_____

_____

_____

_____

_____

_____

_____

_____

Remember your bill of rights. No one has the right to hurt you with words or actions. No one has the right to bully you. No one has the right to destroy your self-worth. Bullying is the death of one's soul. Bullying is destructive. Bullying is an imbalance of power. If you are being bullied, tell someone. If you are a bystander, tell someone. Keep telling until someone listens. Telling is not snitching; it is regaining your power.

Have you ever been a victim of bullying? Have you ever witnessed bullying? Have you ever been a bully? How did you feel? What was the outcome?

We all bleed red!

_____

_____

_____

_____

_____

_____

_____

_____

_____

_____

_____

_____

_____

_____

_____

_____

_____

_____

_____

_____

_____

_____

_____

_____

_____

Draw what respect looks like to you!

Forgiveness

Forgiveness is a conscious decision to let go of anger, hurt, or pain in order to find peace with yourself. Forgiveness doesn't just happen. It takes time. Forgiveness goes through stages: hurt, hate, healing, understanding, and letting go.

Was there a time when you chose to forgive someone? What were you feeling? How did you survive those difficult days? Were you able to tell anybody? Write your story on the following lines. If you need help, find someone you trust to talk to.

_____

_____

_____

_____

_____

_____

_____

_____

_____

_____

_____

_____

_____

_____

_____

_____

_____

_____

_____

_____

_____

_____

_____

_____

_____

_____

_____

_____

_____

_____

_____

_____

Remember that everyone makes mistakes. Quite often, a very remorseful and distressed young person would sit in my office with tears running down his or her cheeks. He or she made a mistake, felt extremely guilty for having done wrong and disappointing so many loved ones, and knew that the past could not be changed. How could anyone forgive the unforgivable?

I found myself repeating these same words over and over. "The word *mistake* is in the dictionary. Webster knew it was important enough to make a definition for it. Everybody makes mistakes, but if you make the same mistake twice, then you are a fool. That word is also in the dictionary!" It gave them a glimpse of hope and made them realize that we are all human. We all make mistakes! Learning from those mistakes and not repeating them is a part of growing up. Many times, the most difficult part of the growth process is being able to forgive oneself.

Write down your thoughts below.

Draw what forgiveness looks like to you!

Happiness

Happiness can only be measured by a person's own definition of happiness. Happiness comes from within. It is that warm feeling that gives you a sense of fulfillment. It puts a smile on your face and a song in your heart. Look deep within to find what makes you happy. Is it reading, drawing, listening to music, hanging out with friends, being with your family, playing sports, or just relaxing? On the lines below, write your own definition of happiness and what makes you happy.

What is your definition of happiness? What makes you happy?

_____

_____

_____

_____

_____

_____

_____

_____

_____

_____

_____

_____

_____

_____

_____

_____

_____

_____

_____

_____

_____

_____

_____

_____

Remember your bill of rights. Life is about making choices. You deserve to be happy. You deserve to love yourself. You deserve to be loved! Can you relate to the following poem, "I Just Want to Be Happy"? What makes this young girl stay in this extremely unhealthy relationship? If you were her friend, what would you say to this confused girl? If you feel this way, please talk to someone. Get the help you need now!

To my friend,

_____
_____
_____
_____
_____
_____
_____
_____
_____
_____
_____
_____
_____
_____
_____
_____
_____
_____
_____

I Just Want to be Happy

I open my door.
There she sits.
Head down.
Eyes drawn.

"Can I talk to you?"
Who is she?
I don't know.
Tears begin to flow.

She speaks softly...slowly.
Trying to understand.
Their relationship is deadly.
She feels trapped.

She can't speak to anyone,
Without his permission!
She can't go anywhere,
Without his permission!
She can't move,
Without his permission!

He texts,
"Where are you?"
"What's wrong?"
"I need to know right now!"

Why does he have to know?
Why should he know
Her every move?
What makes him so controlling?

She's tired of feeling scared.
She's tired of feeling sad.
In a meek and solemn voice,
She cries, "I just want to be happy."

Mrs. D.

208

Draw what happiness looks like to you!

Love

Love is necessary for survival. Love is everlasting. Love is unconditional. Do you love yourself? Please answer this question honestly. If you do love yourself, what makes you answer yes so quickly? If you responded no, what stops you from loving yourself?

Learning to love yourself is like supplying fuel for your soul. You deserve to love yourself. You deserve to receive love. Always remember that you are a beautiful person. You are unique. The eyes that stare back at you in the mirror will always be the same eyes. The heart that beats inside you will always be the same heart. The feelings that you feel will always be your very own feelings.

Today is the first day of the rest of your life. It is time to love yourself. On the lines below, please write what you are feeling right now. Please be honest!

_____

_____

_____

_____

_____

_____

_____

_____

_____

_____

_____

_____

_____

_____

_____

_____

_____

_____

_____

_____

_____

You, yourself, as much as anybody in the entire universe, deserve your love and affection.
—Buddha

Write your thoughts below.

Draw what love looks like to you!

Introspection

The great thing in this world is not so much where you stand, as in what direction you are moving.
—Oliver Wendell Holmes

Introspection speaks to your inner thoughts and emotions. It is divided into two sections. The first segment is devoted to the adolescent. The next portion is dedicated to the adult. It searches deep within to find the real you.

On the pages that follow, please be honest with your answers. Enjoy the moment. When you arrive at "Who Am I?" please allow yourself to write what is in your heart. Take as much time as you need. If you want to skip this section, go ahead. Come back to it when you are ready!

Far away in the sunshine are my highest aspirations. I may not reach them, but I can look up and see their beauty, believe in them, and try to follow where they lead.

—Louisa May Alcott

Me, Myself, and I (Adolescents Only)

Describe your life from childhood to adolescence. What category or categories does it fall under: comedy, tragedy, mystery, or suspense? What have you learned from each event that occurred in your life? How have they affected who you are today? Would you make any changes? Are you happy today? Do you like yourself right now? Can you stop and smell the flowers?

_____

_____

_____

_____

_____

_____

_____

_____

_____

_____

_____

_____

_____

_____

_____

_____

_____

_____

_____

_____

_____

_____

_____

_____

_____

_____

_____

My Favorites (Adolescents Only)

Person_____

Color_____

Song_____

Book_____

TV show_____

Subject_____

Singer/Group_____

Meal/Dessert_____

Car_____

Time of day_____

Season _____

Cologne/perfume_____

Animal_____

Hobby_____

Game_____

Sport _____

Birthday_____

Place _____

Childhood memory_____

Vacation_____

Number_____

Dream_____

Me (Adolescents Only)

My parents/guardians are_____

A dream I hope to fulfill_____

My proudest moment_____

My most embarrassing moment _____

My most memorable childhood experience _____

What I like about me_____

What I dislike about me_____

What I look for in a friend_____

Three things I value the most_____

One word that describes how others view me_____

My prized possession_____

My greatest moment of emotional pain_____

Someone who has impacted my life_____

A teacher who influenced me positively _____

A teacher who influenced me negatively_____

My childhood years were_____

My adolescent years are_____

My best quality_____

My strongest beliefs_____

I am happy when_____

I am sad when_____

I am angry when_____

My Thoughts and Feelings (Adolescents Only)

Addiction_____

Alcohol_____

Friends_____

College_____

Music_____

Dating_____

Death_____

Drugs_____

Boyfriends_____

Family_____

Girlfriends_____

Prejudice_____

Homework_____

Life_____

Prom_____

Teachers_____

Religion_____

Sex_____

Sports_____

Suicide_____

Love_____

Bullying_____

Who Am I? (Freshman Year)

Dear Me,

_____
_____
_____
_____
_____
_____
_____
_____
_____
_____
_____
_____
_____
_____
_____
_____
_____
_____
_____
_____
_____
_____
_____
_____
_____
_____
_____
_____
_____

Who Am I? (Sophomore Year)

Dear Me,

_____

_____

_____

_____

_____

_____

_____

_____

_____

_____

_____

_____

_____

_____

_____

_____

_____

_____

_____

_____

_____

_____

_____

_____

_____

_____

_____

_____

_____

_____

_____

_____

Who Am I? (Junior Year)

Dear Me,

_____
_____
_____
_____
_____
_____
_____
_____
_____
_____
_____
_____
_____
_____
_____
_____
_____
_____
_____
_____
_____
_____
_____
_____
_____
_____
_____
_____
_____
_____
_____
_____
_____
_____
_____

Who Am I? (Senior Year)

Dear Me,

_____
_____
_____
_____
_____
_____
_____
_____
_____
_____
_____
_____
_____
_____
_____
_____
_____
_____
_____
_____
_____
_____
_____
_____
_____
_____
_____
_____
_____
_____
_____
_____
_____

Who Am I? (After High School)

Dear Me,

_____

_____

_____

_____

_____

_____

_____

_____

_____

_____

_____

_____

_____

_____

_____

_____

_____

_____

_____

_____

_____

_____

_____

_____

_____

_____

_____

_____

_____

_____

_____

_____

To My Parent/Guardian

Dear _____,

_____

_____

_____

_____

_____

_____

_____

_____

_____

_____

_____

_____

_____

_____

_____

_____

_____

_____

_____

_____

_____

_____

_____

_____

_____

_____

_____

_____

_____

_____

_____

_____

_____

_____

_____

To My Teacher

Dear _____,

Me, Myself, and I (Parents/Guardians and Teachers Only)

Describe your life from childhood to adolescence. What category or categories does it fall under: comedy, tragedy, mystery, or suspense? What have you learned from each event that occurred in your life? How have they affected who you are today? Would you make any changes? Are you happy today? Do you like yourself right now? Can you stop and smell the flowers?

_____

_____

_____

_____

_____

_____

_____

_____

_____

_____

_____

_____

_____

_____

_____

_____

_____

_____

_____

_____

_____

_____

_____

_____

_____

_____

I.12BME

My Favorite (Parents/Guardians and Teachers Only)

Person_____

Color_____

Song_____

Book_____

TV show_____

Subject_____

Singer/Group_____

Meal/Dessert_____

Car_____

Time of day_____

Season _____

Cologne/perfume_____

Animal_____

Hobby_____

Game_____

Sport _____

Birthday_____

Place _____

Childhood memory_____

Vacation_____

Number_____

Dream_____

Me (Parents/Guardians and Teachers Only)

My parents/guardians are_____

A dream I hope to fulfill_____

My proudest moment_____

My most embarrassing moment_____

My most memorable childhood experience _____

What I like about me _____

What I dislike about me_____

What I look for in a friend_____

Three things I value the most_____

One word that describes how others view me_____

My prized possession_____

My greatest moment of emotional pain_____

Someone who has impacted my life_____

A teacher who influenced me positively _____

My adult years are_____

My childhood years were_____

My adolescent years were _____

My best quality_____

My strongest beliefs_____

I am happy when_____

I am sad when_____

I am angry when_____

My Thoughts and Feelings (Parents/Guardians and Teachers Only)

Alcohol_____

Drugs_____

School_____

Work_____

Dating_____

Death_____

Music_____

Vacation_____

Family_____

War_____

Politics_____

Sports_____

Environment_____

Animals_____

Computers_____

Addiction_____

Prejudice_____

Suicide_____

Religion_____

Parents_____

Teachers_____

Life_____

Who Am I? (Childhood Years)

Dear Me,

_____
_____
_____
_____
_____
_____
_____
_____
_____
_____
_____
_____
_____
_____
_____
_____
_____
_____
_____
_____
_____
_____
_____
_____
_____
_____
_____
_____
_____

I12BME

Who Am I? (Adolescent Years)

Dear Me,

_____

_____

_____

_____

_____

_____

_____

_____

_____

_____

_____

_____

_____

_____

_____

_____

_____

_____

_____

_____

_____

_____

_____

_____

_____

_____

_____

_____

_____

Who Am I? (Adult Years)

Dear Me,

_____

_____

_____

_____

_____

_____

_____

_____

_____

_____

_____

_____

_____

_____

_____

_____

_____

_____

_____

_____

_____

_____

_____

_____

_____

_____

_____

_____

_____

_____

_____

_____

To My Child

Dear _____,

_____

_____

_____

_____

_____

_____

_____

_____

_____

_____

_____

_____

_____

_____

_____

_____

_____

_____

_____

_____

_____

_____

_____

_____

_____

_____

_____

_____

_____

_____

_____

_____

To My Student

Dear _____,

_____
_____
_____
_____
_____
_____
_____
_____
_____
_____
_____
_____
_____
_____
_____
_____
_____
_____
_____
_____
_____
_____
_____
_____
_____
_____
_____
_____
_____
_____

Me, Myself, and I (Adolescents, Parents/Guardians, and Teachers)

Years ago, I created the license plate I12BME for my own personal use. It remains with me until this day. In the mirror below, design your very own personal license plate that reflects who you are as a person. There are no guidelines. Be creative!

Part 3

Afterthoughts:
Words Written from the Heart

Hope is the thing with feathers that perches in the soul.
—Emily Dickinson

The following pages contain a collection of poetry and prose written by me to students, parents/guardians, and you. The written word can have a greater impact than the spoken word.

Trust thyself; every heart vibrates to that iron string.
—Ralph Waldo Emerson

Listen to Your Heart ... Your Inner Voice

As this young girl searches for answers to life's most difficult questions, she feels overwhelmed until she hears a voice.

Heart
Only five letters
Two vowels
Three consonants
One syllable
The main organ
Keeps one alive
One beat at a time
Uninterrupted
Look inside ... he*art*
Three letters
Two vowels
One syllable ... ear
Listen to your heart
Hear the voice
Whose voice ... your voice
Hear what your heart is saying.
I'm scared
Fear consumes ... heart races
A gentle tear falls
Help me.
I am always near
Day after day, year after year
Hear me
Do not fear me
Feel me beating
Hear my thoughts
Search deep inside
Dear heart ... I hear you.

Day 3: Alone

These words are for every teenager who is in the midst of a breakup. Love hurts. Today is day three of heartache.

Eyes tired,
Tired of crying,
A heavy heart.
Was it love?
I thought it was love.
No, it was love.
We are young.
Allow time to heal.
Words of wisdom.
I hear them.
I do not feel them.
It hurts so bad.
What was it?
It was different.
I believed.
Emptiness,
I am so confused.
Day three: alone.

Someday You Will Find the Answers

An extremely intelligent, independent, and sensitive young girl abandoned by her mother at the age of five searches for the lost child within.

Those sad, tender young eyes,
deep brown pools of darkness
staring into the distance,
That soft, innocent voice
looking for the answers
to life's greatest mysteries.
Who am I?
Where am I?
The lost child
Someday
you will have answers.
Someday
you will want to trust.
Someday
you will understand.
Someday
you will give yourself
permission
to erupt,
to explode,
allowing your thoughts and
emotions to surface.
Emptiness and loneliness
will fade away
And then good-bye,
wall of silence.

Diagnosis: Cancer

This fourteen-year-old wipes the tears from her eyes as she speaks about her grandfather's diagnosis. She respects his wishes. She will not go to the hospital. She will remember him healthy, smiling, and alive.

Cancer creating chaos
within—
deadly, darkening disease
uninvited,
stealing slithering sloth
destroying.
The fight begins …
sunshine sneaking steadily
inside,
holding hearts hopeful
united,
living life lovingly,
surviving.
The fight goes on!

With love in his heart and tears in his eyes, this seventeen-year-old finds the strength to speak to his mother about the day that changed his life forever. That day changed his family forever and has held him captive forever. It is time to let go. It is time to move on. It is time to accept the truth.

Dear Mom,

When I was only seven years old, you said, "Everything is going to be okay." Then why did I feel so scared? You told me that our family would always stay together. Then why did Dad stop coming home at night?

You said, "Don't worry. I love you." Then why did you look so sad? I felt it then. It was that horrible feeling … that sad feeling … that sick feeling … that deep in the gut feeling. I felt it then. Something was wrong.

"Help!" I cried silently to myself. I tried desperately to keep that smile on my face.

Ten years have passed. I am still crying on the inside. I am still smiling on the outside. You continue to tell me that everything will be okay. It isn't. You pretend that our family is still together. We aren't. You tell me that it's nobody's business. It isn't.

"There is nothing to be ashamed of, Mom." Our family has been torn apart. It was Dad who chose to leave. It is not my fault. It is not your fault.

"Everything is going to be okay." We will always be together. "Don't worry, Mom. I love you."

It's time to face the truth. It's time to stop pretending. It's time for acceptance. It's time to live again—happily ever after!

Love forever,
Your son

Sexually abused by her stepfather, this beautiful, brown-eyed fifteen-year-old girl struggles to live one day at a time.

Fifteen Years Old

The world on
her shoulders—
life isn't fair.
Expect nothing.
Get nothing.
Why so negative?
ABUSED
Four years old
Five years old
Six years old
Seven years old
Eight years old
Nine years old
Ten years old
Eleven years old
Twelve years old
Why so angry?
Feelings numbed,
body and mind
separated
for survival.
When can healing
begin?
Today,
if she allows it.

The Secret Is Out

A very humble parent shared her story with me to give hope to any young person who is facing physical or mental abuse. No one has a right to abuse you. No one has the right to destroy you. You have the power within you to stop being abused. You are not alone. Please get the help you need. Please tell someone!

I was just a young girl,
Loving life,
When you stole a part of me.
My innocence … my youth.
Playing your game,
Following your rules.
The stakes were high,
Lots of pennies for me.
And in return,
Pleasure for you.
I remember those words:
"It's our secret."
Who were you kidding?
It was blackmail.
It was your secret.
Your sickness.
A selfish, disgusting act,
Meant to gratify only you.
You … a man I've grown to hate
A hatred that has consumed me
For forty years.
Repressed deep within,
Only to surface today.
I trusted you.
I loved you.
I respected you.
You were my family.
You were my blood
And now,
You are nothing.
Nothing to me.
The secret is out … I am free
The game is over!

Forty years have passed since her teenaged uncle abused her. Vowing to keep it a secret from her mother and choosing to keep the family intact, she never told anyone—until today. Today she buried her mother. The secret is out. She is free!

A Second Chance

Seven days have passed since the phone rang last Friday morning. A young girl cries hysterically as she tells me that her boyfriend has been rushed to the hospital. He took some pills. He may have to go on life support. She asks me if I know why. Why would the boy she loves try to end his life? Only he knows why, and today he has a second chance to live—and to answer the question why.

One week ago …
Overdose
Oxygen
Sleep
Stillness
Today …
Breathing
Awake
Movement
Life
One week ago …
Overdose
Darkness
Silence
Tears
Today …
Light
Truth
Hope
Life
A second chance … to live!

It Always Seems Like Yesterday

Six years after her father's death, this soft-spoken girl sat with a classmate whose mother had just passed away. When he told her that his mother had died the day before, she looked at him, smiled, and quietly remarked, "It always seems like yesterday."

Dying is
so final,
so real,
so sad.
Yet it always seems like yesterday.
Minutes pass,
days pass,
hours pass,
years pass.
Yet it always seems like yesterday.
Sun rises,
sun sets,
she laughs,
she cries.
Yet it always seems like yesterday.
Just ten years old
when Daddy died.
It stings;
it numbs.
Yet it always seems like yesterday.
Memories
of love,
sweet sixteen—
painful.
Yet it always seems like yesterday.
Sun rises,
sun sets,
she laughs,
she cries.
Yet it always seems like yesterday.
Dying is
so final,
so real,
so sad.
I love you, Daddy.

A Letter from Pop

A year and a half has gone by since the death of his grandfather, and this extremely distraught fifteen-year-old is finding it difficult to move forward. He is angry. He is sad. He is upset that he never got to say good-bye to his grandfather. He was finally able to write a good-bye letter to Pop. It was the first time that he cried since his grandfather's death. He thanked him for teaching him about life. He thanked him for giving him a great appreciation for music and dancing. He thanked him for being the greatest role model in the world! The following is Pop's response to this precious letter that can be found on page 38.

Dear Grandson,

I received your letter today. It brought tears to my eyes. I am so proud of you. I miss you too. I love you. Please know that I am at peace. It is time for you to find peace. Although we are apart, always remember I am with you forever. I am a part of you. I am in your heart. I am in your soul! Letting go doesn't mean forgetting. It means remembering … remembering all the great times we had together … remembering all the laughter we shared … remembering all the memories we created. Love lives on. Love never ends.

Below is a poem I wrote just for you. Keep it in my socks that you tucked away in your drawer the day I left you. Remember these words forever, especially when you are dancing!

I see the smile on your face
each time you speak my name.
I taste the tears that flow from your eyes
each time you speak my name.
I hear the love in your voice
each time you speak my name.
I feel the weight of your soul
each time you speak my name.
The time has come to let me go
so I can rest in peace.
The time has come to let me go
so you can live again.
Don't be afraid.
I am with you forever.
I love you!

Love,
Pop

A Synopsis of Life Using Drugs

If life with drugs mirrors life without drugs, what's the big deal? What's wrong with drinking and using drugs? Speak to an adolescent who has lived his or her high school years using drugs. Speak to the parents of that high school student who made the choice to use drugs. Their stories are all the same. They all live the same nightmare. The characters change, but the plot remains the same. The ending is always unknown!

Please read the following poem if you are thinking about experimenting with drugs. I wrote it several years ago when I counseled one of my students who chose to use drugs. Years have gone by, and each time I am faced with counseling a young person who is caught up in the drug world, I find myself repeating the same words.

No feelings … no emotions
No family … no real friends
No money
No me
Just drugs
Good versus evil
Darkness … deceit … danger
Inner turmoil
Struggling
Scared
Lonely
Where am I?
Life
Death
Choices
Who am I?

Confused People

One sunny spring afternoon I received a note in my mailbox from a very special girl. "Hi, Mrs. D. I need to talk to you about my Pre-Calculus grade. I need some guidance. Please call me down when you have a minute."

Within moments, she appeared at my door with two friends. We talked about the level of difficulty of the class. We talked about solutions to her problem. We talked about getting extra help. We talked about the consequences of receiving a low grade. We talked about how lousy she felt. We talked about how her parents viewed the situation.

With sadness in her voice, she told me that her car was taken away because she got a C in Pre-Calculus. Very innocently, she said, "Parents are confused people."

If she always receives good grades and is a good student and never gets into trouble, why did her parents punish her? She was already punishing herself. Why did they have to punish her too? She was confused about the way they were thinking.

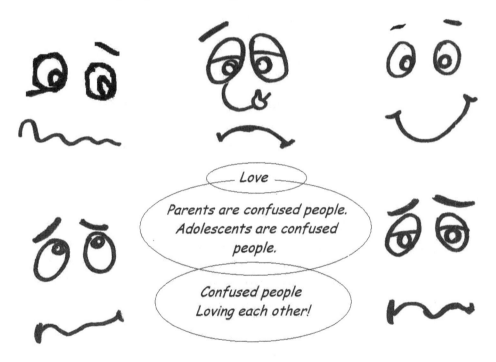

Let Me Fly Alone (for a While)

Adolescence is a time of letting go and becoming independent.

You've given me the power to choose.
You've given me the wisdom to grow.
You've given me wings to fly.
And now the time has come
For me to break free.
Don't be scared.
You are always with me.
I will be okay.
Please
Let me fly alone for a while
Into the unknown
To ask my own questions.
Please
Let me fly alone for a while
Into the unknown
To find my own answers.
Please
Let me fly alone for a while
Into the unknown
To make my own mistakes.
Please
Let me fly alone for a while
Into the unknown
To discover who I am.
And when it's time for me to
Come back home,
Let me thank you for believing in me
And trusting me to fly alone
For just a while.
I love you!

I Love You, My Child

Below is a poem written to every parent/guardian who has faced the greatest responsibility in life: raising a child. A child comes with no directions and no manual—just unconditional love!

I began the role of parent with my own expectations,
my own wants and needs, my own fears and worries.
I have raised you with strong morals and beliefs.
I have taught you right from wrong.
I have but three wishes for you—
independence, health, happiness.
I know that communication is crucial
to our existence during these difficult years.
I promise to listen to you, and in return,
I ask you to please listen to me.
As we face adolescence together,
always remember …
I am your parent. I love you, my child.
I will remain in control even when you have lost control.
I am your parent. I love you, my child.
I will stick to my values and beliefs even when you have forgotten what you believe in.
I am your parent. I love you, my child.
I will listen to my inner voice even when your inner voice is silenced.
I am your parent. I love you, my child.
I will keep the door open even when you slam the door shut.
I am your parent. I love you, my child.
I will continue to believe in you even when you no longer believe in yourself.
And as adolescence ends, may these three wishes come true—
independence, health, happiness.
I am your parent.
I love you, my child—forever!

I am larger, better than I thought; I did not know I held so much goodness.
—Walt Whitman

Reflections

Thank you from the bottom of my heart!

♡ Mrs. D.

Please share your thoughts...

myafterthoughts@mail.com

Each day I try to understand why I had such a yearning desire to write *Tell Me a Story about This Crazy World Called High School*. As I search for an answer, I realize that on a daily basis, I am consumed with so many private and powerful feelings. These feelings belong to hundreds of young, innocent adolescents. These feelings are so much a part of growing up. If these feelings are bottled up inside, they can destroy a person. If they are let go, they can heal a person.

Feelings are real. No one has the right to negate them. They truly exist. I am the stranger who listens empathetically and without judgment. Sharing these stories helps heal my heart and allows me to continue on my life's journey.

I am ready for the next young person to walk through my door. I am ready for that next story to be unraveled. I am ready for that next vulnerable human being to trust me unconditionally and allow me to look so deeply into his or her eyes and see into the window of the soul.

It humbles me to be given such a great task in life. From my heart to yours, thank you for trusting me.

With love,
Mrs. D.

About the Author

Mrs. D. is a counselor who lives in New Jersey with her husband, children, and grandchildren. The transition from elementary teacher to high school counselor sparked the makings of *Tell Me a Story about This Crazy World Called High School*. As a counselor, she quickly discovered that the written word is an extremely powerful tool for healing the soul. Mrs. D. previously published a journal titled *Afterthoughts: Words Written from the Heart for Adolescents and Parents/Guardians*.

About the Illustrator

Tara Balboa is a mother of two beautiful young children and currently resides in New Jersey. She studied fine arts at the School of Visual Arts in Manhattan, receiving her BFA upon graduation in 2007. *Tell Me a Story about This Crazy World Called High School* is her second published work.

Works Cited

"48 Calming Buddha Quotes," *Famous Quotes Love Quotes Inspirational Quotes QuotesNSmiles. com.* N.p., n.d. Web. 03 July 2015.

Alcott, Louisa May. *Work: A Story of Experience.* Thorndike Press, 1873.

Brain, Jennifer, and Louisa May Alcott. *Little Women.* Oxford: Oxford UP, 1979.

Confucius, and David H. Li. *The Analects of Confucius: A New-Millennium Translation.* Bethesda, MD: Premier Pub., 1999.

Dickinson, Emily, and Ralph William Franklin. *The Poems of Emily Dickinson.* Cambridge, Mass.: Belknap of Harvard U, 1998.

Emerson, Ralph Waldo, and Brooks Atkinson. *The Complete Essays and Other Writings of Ralph Waldo Emerson.* New York: Modern Library, 1940.

Laozi, Hua – Ching, Ni. *The Complete Works of Lao Tzu: Tao the Ching and Hua Hu Ching.* Santa Monica: Seven Star Communications, 1995.

Merriam-Webster. *Merriam-Webster,* n.d. Web. 10 July 2015.

"Oliver Wendell Holmes Sr. Quotes." Oliver Wendell Holmes Sr. Quotes (Author of *Autocrat of the Breakfast Table*). N.p., n.d. Web. 03 July 2015.

"The Quotations Page: Quote from Chinese Proverb." The Quotations Page. N.p., n.d. Web. 03 July 2015.

"Robert Browning Quotes." Robert Browning Quotes (Author of "My Last Duchess and Other Poems"). N.p., n.d. Web. 04 July 2015.

"Samuel Johnson Quote." A–Z Quotes. N.p., n.d. Web. 08 July 2015.

Whitman, Walt. *Leaves of Grass.* New York: Vintage/Library of America, 1992.

"World of Proverbs—Famous Quotes: Just When the Caterpillar Thought the World Was Over, It Became a Butterfly. English Proverb [19620]." World of Proverbs—Famous Quotes: Just When the Caterpillar Thought the World Was Over, It Became a Butterfly. English Proverb [19620]. N.p., n.d. Web. 03 July 2015.

Resources

National AIDS Hotline: 1-800-232-4636

National Association of Anorexia Nervosa and Associated Disorders (ANAD): 630-577-1330

National Cancer Information Service: 1-800-422-6237

National Child Abuse Hotline: 1-800-4-A-CHILD (422.4453) or 800-2-A-CHILD (222.4453, TDD for hearing impaired)

National Domestic Violence/Child Abuse/Sexual Abuse: 1-800-799-SAFE (7233)/800-787-3224 TDD

National Drug Information Treatment and Referral Hotline: 1-800-662-HELP (4357)

National Parent Hotline: 1-800-840-6537

Nationwide RAINN National Rape Crisis Hotline: 1-800-656-4673

National Suicide Prevention Hotline: 1-800-SUICIDE/1-800-784-2433

National Youth Crisis Hotline: 1-800-442-HOPE (4673)

Recommended Readings

Andrews, Andy. *The Noticer.* Thomas Nelson, 2009.

Armour, Vernice. *Zero to Breakthrough.* Gotham Books, 2011.

Blanco, Jodee. *Please Stop Laughing at Me.* Adams Media Corporation, 2003.

Buscaglia, Leo. *Personhood.* Fawcett Columbine, 1978.

Canfield, J., Hansen, M. V., Kirberger, K. *Chicken Soup for the Teenage Soul.* Health Communications, 1997.

Carlson, Melody. *Diary of a Teenage Girl.* Multnomah Publishers, 2000.

Carter-Scott, Cherie. *If Life Is a Game, These are the Rules.* Broadway Books, 1998.

Coelho, Paul. *The Alchemist.* Harper One, 1993.

Dellasega, Cheryl, PhD. *Surviving Ophelia.* Ballantine Books, 2001.

Earl, Esther. *This Star Won't Go Out.* Dutton Books, 2014.

Ford, Amanda. *Be True to Yourself.* Conari Press, 2000.

Gordon, Jon. *The Energy Bus.* John Wiley & Son, Inc., 2007.

Gottlieb, Lori. *Stick Figure.* Berkeley Books, 2000.

Green, John. *The Fault in Our Stars.* Penguin Books, 2012.

Graham, Stedman. *Teens Can Make It Happen Workbook.* Fireside, 2001.

Hesse, Hermann. *Demian.* Perennial Classics, 1925.

Hornbacher, Marya. *Wasted: A Memoir of Anorexia and Bulimia.* Harper Perennial, 1998.

Johnson, Spencer. *The Precious Present.* Bantam Doubleday Dell Publishing Group, 1992.

Keel, Philipp. *All about Me.* Ballantine Books, 1998.

Knapp, Caroline. *Drinking: A Love Story.* Delta, 1996.

Kubler-Ross, Elisabeth. *On Death and Dying.* Touchstone Books, 1969.

Kundtz, David. *Quiet Mind.* Conari Press, 2000.

Levenkron, Steven. *Cutting.* W.W. Norton and Co., 1998.

Maslow, Abraham. *Toward a Psychology of Being.* John Wiley and Sons, Inc., 1999.

Millman, Dan. *The Journeys of Socrates.* Harper Collins, 2005.

Millman, Dan. *The Peaceful Warrior.* MJK, 1984.

Nelson, Jane EdD, and Lynn Lott. *Positive Discipline for Teenagers.* Prima, 2000.

Oher, Michael. *I Beat The Odds: From Homelessness to the Blind Side and Beyond.* Gotham, 2012.

Omartian, Stormie. *Just Enough Light for the Step I'm On.* Harvest House, 1999.

Paulus, Trina. *Hope for the Flowers.* Paulist Press, 1972.

Peale, Norman Vincent. *The Power of Positive Thinking.* Fawcett Crest, 1952.

Peck, M. Scott, MD. *The Road Less Traveled.* Simon and Schuster, 1978.

Pelzer, David. *The Child Called It.* Health Communications, 1995.

Pipher, Mary PhD. *Reviving Ophelia.* Ballantine Books, 1994.

Ramos, Karim. *From Fat Farm to Phat Farm.* Xlibris Corporation, 2010.

Ryan, M. J. *Attitudes of Gratitudes.* MJF Books, 1999.

Sanchez, Alex. *Rainbow Boys.* Simon and Schuster, 2001.

Sanders, Mark D. and Tia Sillers. *Climb.* Rutledge Hill Press, 2003.

Sanders, Mark D. and Tia Sillers. *I Hope You Dance.* Rutledge Hill Press, 2000.

Schroff, Laura and Tresniowski, Alex. *An Invisible Thread.* Howard Books, 2011.

Seligman, Martin E. P., PhD. *Authentic Happiness.* Free Press, 2002.

Shandler, Sara. *Ophelia Speaks.* Harper Perennial, 1999.

Simmons, Rachel. *Odd Girl Out.* Harcourt Books, 2002.

Simon, Lizzie. *Detour.* Atria Books, 2002.

Stepanek, Mattie J. T. *Reflections of a Peacemaker.* Andrews McMeel, 2005.

Toma, David. *Toma Tells It Straight with Love.* Books in Focus, 1981.

Twerski, Abraham. *Addictive Thinking: Understanding Self-Deception.* Hazelden, 1997.

Urban, Hal. *Life's Greatest Lessons.* Simon and Schuster Trade, 2002.

Walls, Jeannette. *The Glass Castle.* Simon and Schuster Trade, 2006.

Index

114, 130, 152, 168, 176

frustration, 64, 70

future, 22, 76, 130, 140, 152, 168, 170

G

gay, being, 122

graduates

    describing who you are, 222

    stories from, 158–177

gratitude, 64, 132, 142, 144

grief, 38, 112, 118, 132, 142, 160, 172, 198–200, 246, 247

guilt, 82, 84, 205

H

hanging on, 170

happiness, 3, 42, 44, 50, 52, 76, 88, 92, 98, 150, 182, 194, 207–209, 242, 251

"Happy Ever After," 242

harassment, dealing with, 72, 88, 190. *See also* abuse; bullying

"Hard to Go On," 160

having fun, consequences of not doing well in school, 124

"Healing from the Inside Out," 243

health issues, dealing with, 172, 174, 176, 241. *See also* cancer

heart, listening to, ix, 3, 34, 40, 213, 238

heartbroken/heart aches, 94, 122, 126, 130, 170, 174, 198, 239, 253

Holmes, Oliver Wendell, 213

hope, vii, ix, 3, 18, 64, 88, 92, 122, 132, 152, 198, 205, 236, 241, 244, 245

"Hope in the Depths of My Heart," 64

hotlines, 259

I

"I Believe," 18

"I Just Want to be Happy," 208

"I Love You, My Child," 251

if statements, 196

illness, 198. *See also* cancer; health issues

independent

    becoming, 132, 162, 182, 240, 250, 251

    feeling, 120

inner voice, vii, 238, 251

insight, 26, 30, 46

inspirational quotes

    Alcott, Louisa May, 180, 213

    Browning, Robert, 194

    Buddha, 211

    Confucius, xv

    Dickinson, Emily, 236

    Emerson, Ralph Waldo, 237

    Holmes, Oliver Wendell, 213

    Johnson, Samuel, xi

    Lao Tzu, 2, 194

    Whitman, Walt, 252

introspection, 213–252

"It Always Seems Like Yesterday," 246

It's Not Real Until You Write It Down, 172

J

"The Jimmy Chronicles," 100, 102, 104

Johnson, Samuel, xi

joy, 20, 134

junior year

    describing who you are, 220

    stories from students about, 56–105

K

knowing yourself, 98, 150

L

Lao Tzu, 2, 194

"Let Me Fly Alone (for a While)," 250

"A Letter from Pop," 247

letting go, 118, 182, 204, 242, 247, 250, 253. *See also* moving on

license plate, personal, 234

"Life," 30

life

    describing yours, 214, 216

    meaning of, 195–197

    parents/guardians describing theirs, 227

    teachers describing theirs, 227

"Life's Toughest Questions," 194–212

"Listen to Your Heart ... Your Inner Voice," 238

loneliness, 82, 84, 108, 112

loss, 112, 116, 118, 160, 198–200. *See also* death,

"Just when the caterpillar thought the world was over, it became a butterfly!"

Anonymous

Printed in the United States
By Bookmasters